THE LAWYER'S GUIDE TO
Marketing
on the
Internet

Gregory H. Siskind
and
Deborah McMurray

**ABALAW
PRACTICE
DIVISION**
The Business of Practicing Law

Cover design by Lachina

Printed in the United States of America.

21 20 19 18 17 5 4 3 2 1

Library of Congress Cataloging-in-Publication Data
Names: McMurray, Deborah, author. | Siskind, Gregory H., author.
Title: The lawyer's guide to marketing on the internet / Deborah McMurray
  and Greg Siskind.
Description: Fourth Edition | Chicago : American Bar Association, 2017. |
  Includes index.
Identifiers: LCCN 2017000373 | ISBN 9781634257374 (print)
Subjects: LCSH: Lawyers—United States—Marketing. | Law firms—United States—Marketing. |
  Internet marketing—United States.
Classification: LCC KF316.5 .S57 2017 | DDC 340.068/8—dc23
LC record available at https://lccn.loc.gov/2017000373

www.ShopABA.org

Table of Contents

Chapter 17: The Ethics of Client Development on the Internet and through Social Media
David Hricik

About the Authors

Greg Siskind has practiced immigration law since 1990 and created Visalaw.com in 1994 for his new law practice. It was one of the very first law firm websites and the experience of creating that site was what inspired him to co-author the original edition of *The Lawyers Guide to Marketing on the Internet*, published in 1996. In 1997, he created the first lawyer blog and recently he was named by ABC News as one of the top 20 people to follow on Twitter to keep up on the immigration debate. Mr. Siskind is the author of several other books, including the annually published *J-1 Visa Guidebook*, *The Employer's Immigration Compliance Desk Reference*, and *The Physician Immigration Handbook*. He primarily practices in business and employment immigration law and directs technology initiatives for his law firm, Siskind Susser.

Deborah McMurray is the founder, chief executive officer, and strategy architect of Content Pilot LLC, a strategy, design, content, and technology company that serves law firms and other professional services firms. Clients include the world's largest law firms, regional powerhouses, and local boutiques—all firms that want better websites and business development strategies and tools. Prior to Content Pilot, Deborah created and led the marketing departments at two large Texas firms for 11 years, then established a successful consultancy. She is known as an expert in strategy-driven web design, an evangelist for successful experience management initiatives, and a leader in developing smarter, better, and more intuitive proposal automation tools that get law firms closer to their buyers of legal services.

Deborah was inducted into the Legal Marketing Hall of Fame in 2008, was elected into the College of Law Practice Management in 2007, and was named as one of *National Law Journal*'s "2013 Top 50 Legal Business Trailblazers & Pioneers." In the past year, Deborah has spoken at the international conferences for Meritas, the Legal Marketing Association, the Association of Legal Administrators, and the International Legal Technology Association, as well as numerous chapter and regional conferences for these organizations. She is also a voracious writer (including her most recent white paper, "How Do They Measure Up? 2016 AmLaw Global 50 Websites: Ten Foundational Best Practices," two prior editions of this book, and the popular 2004 book *The Lawyer's Guide to Marketing*, of which she was co-editor)—catch more of her thinking on her Law Firm 4.0 Blog.

Acknowledgments

The authors would like to thank the many people who have helped make this fourth edition of *The Lawyers Guide to Marketing on the Internet* possible. In particular, we would like to thank David Hricik and Tim Stanley, who contributed their expertise to the project by authoring the chapters on ethics and search engine optimization. We would also like to thank all of the people at the American Bar Association who helped us through the writing and editorial process. In particular, Carole Levitt, Tom Mighell, and Tim Stanley, who provided many helpful comments and suggestions that have made our book considerably better.

Finally, we would like to thank our friends and family. Greg would like to thank, in particular, his wife, Audrey Siskind, for her support and his law partner, Lynn Susser, who has been willing to give Greg's crazy technology and marketing ideas a shot for the past 22 years. Deborah would like to thank her terrific colleagues at Content Pilot, the numerous colleagues who are interviewed or otherwise contributed smart advice in this book: Paul Bonner, Leigh Dance, Adrian Dayton, Eric Fletcher, Allen Fuqua, Richard Hsu, Elizabeth Lampert, Norm Rubenstein, Elonide Semmes, Adam Stock, Oliver Thoenen, and Keith Wewe. Plus—she thanks her wonderful husband, Glen Davison, for his abiding support and love.

Introduction to this Fourth Edition

The cataclysmic changes that have occurred on the Internet and how we access it since we published our last book in 2007 are almost as earth-shattering as the very start of the Internet itself. The first book was published in 1996, our second in 2002, and our third in 2007. Before 1996, no lawyer imagined that the Internet would transform our personal and professional lives—and certainly could not fathom that it would change the practice of law and have any impact at all on buyers of legal services or how those services would be delivered. My co-author, Greg Siskind, wrote that revolutionary first book because he was the first solo practitioner and first immigration lawyer in the United States to build and launch a website.

For example, in 1996, the year I was tasked to build my then law firm's first website (I was its marketing director), the managing partner of my firm said, "Don't spend a lot of time on it—the Internet is *not* here to stay. Serious business lawyers should never stoop so low."

Most of the writing of our last book occurred in 2006, and it hit the shelves in the spring of 2007. *Before* Apple introduced the iPhone and *before* anyone understood the term "social media." Blogs were becoming popular, but they were not widespread for lawyers or easy for non-technical people to design and launch.

Internet marketing for lawyers has mushroomed in ways we could not have envisioned. Lawyers did not have YouTube channels, Twitter handles and leagues of followers, hundreds of LinkedIn comrades, or Facebook pages that they actually want people to view.

Also, the iPhone and other smartphone creators set off a firestorm of easy, intuitive, graphically interesting, and fun features, which enabled lawyers and their buyers to read e-mail, texts, and articles, watch videos, share photos, and connect on social media while waiting in traffic, commuting by train—pretty much doing anything, 24/7. A majority of us are addicted to our phones and tablets and we use them as much during our business day as we do to facilitate our personal lives. The lines are blurred beyond recognition.

Yet, in 2016, there are still lawyers and firms that do not have a website or any social media presence. Perhaps they also still carry flip phones. It is hard to find statistics about the number of lawyers who do not subscribe to Internet marketing of any variety (because they are nearly invisible), but I did find a December 2014 blog post written by Lawyers Mutual Insurance Company called "Why Have a Website?" Here is how it starts:

> Today I wanted to hire a lawyer. I looked up 13 lawyers by name and couldn't find websites for 9 of them. How do you expect people to find you without a website?
>
> For most of the 9 lawyers, I did find a generic listing on a website such as yellowpages.com, lawyers.com or yelp.com, however, I didn't take those lawyers seriously and many potential clients may not either. For one thing, I was looking for a lawyer with a specific skill set. I'm not sure the yelp review is the best way to determine that you have the skills I need.
>
> What holds lawyers back from creating websites? The top 3 reasons are lack of technical knowledge, concern about the cost of the website and the time spent learning about the technology and then creating the content for the website.

Because buyers of legal services are Internet savvy, they expect their lawyers to be as well. This book is designed for both sophisticated Internet marketers and lawyers who are ready to jump into it. Not every strategy and tactic will make sense for you, your audiences, or your firm. Evaluate the ideas against your goals and choose those that will get you closest to achieving them.

Deborah McMurray

Developing an Internet Marketing Plan

"Internet marketing" is a very broad field with an increasingly expansive list of options and components. One enormous advantage over traditional offline marketing and media is reach. With the vastness of the Internet combined with well-thought-out plans and the right tools, you have the potential of reaching audiences on all seven continents.

That enormous scope, however, can also be a downside. Unless yours is a global law firm and your practice is international, you do not need to reach potential clients in Australia, Asia, or Antarctica. The first and most critical step in your Internet marketing plan is to define your audiences and narrow your reach. Your audiences and practice mix will inform what Internet tools and media will make the most sense for you. Unless you have a team of Internet marketers devoted to you and your practice, you cannot and should not try to exploit all that is available to you. Where are your buyers spending their time? Focus on showing up there.

While this book will cover the most popular tools available, we start with what we deem the foundational tool—the most important one—the website. As you will learn later in this book, buyers of legal services really do validate referrals and evaluate your strengths on your website—long before you even know they are checking you out. Having a smart, well-designed website is imperative today.

MILLIONS OF DOLLARS are spent on law firm website design and development each year. Still today, the process is often without discipline, resulting in significant scope creep and sky-rocketing, out-of-control budgets. And, every day, websites are launched that look and feel "cookie cutter"—they are not strategic, tailored to the specific law firm client base or culture, and are not giving visitors what they want and need. In other words, they are not working very hard for the sponsoring law firms. These firms have a web "presence," but not a very hard-working one.

An undisciplined planning process results in experimentation, guesswork, and random decision making. This means that the needs of your important visitors are taking a backseat to the internal politics that often are at the center of these important initiatives.

Designing and building a website without a strategic plan that establishes and prioritizes goals is akin to building a house without any architectural blueprints. And it can often cost the same amount of money!

Use the suggestions in this chapter to develop a go-to-market plan and lock in your strategy and scope before you spend one dollar on your next generation site.

ANALYZE YOUR FIRM TO DEVELOP YOUR INTERNET MARKETING PLAN

Your Firm's Business Strategy

Every law firm, regardless of size, requires a strategy to help lawyers to focus. Without focus there is no leverage. And without leverage, you will find yourself needlessly repeating, forgetting, and misplacing things that are critical to running a successful practice. *You will never make as much money without a strategy as you will with one.*

When it comes to your firm's website, visitors want to know what they should think about you. They do not know what to think—even if they are familiar with your firm. Do not assume they know or remember anything about you.

If you are not sure where to begin, start with simple questions.

Answer these three questions and you will be on your way to developing your Internet marketing plan. Below are other simple questions so you can plan more specifically.

Questions to ask yourself to develop your Internet marketing plan

What Are Your Firm's Top Skills?
And Who Are Your Clients?

- Analyze your practice—be specific. Who are your clients today, and whom do you want as clients in the future? What are their industries? Who are your clients' customers?
- How will your practice and clients change over the next five years?
- How will your clients' companies and industries change over the next five years (regulation, deregulation, consolidation, globalization)?
- What are the important problems your clients face? What keeps them awake at night?
- What top skills in your firm help them solve their most pressing problems and address their best opportunities?

What Do Clients Need Help With?

Hundreds of interviews with business-to-business buyers of legal services prove that they self-identify first as a member of an industry—say energy or healthcare. Your prospect views herself as a human resources professional in the energy industry, working for a midstream independent. All that before she ponders having an employment problem related to trade secret theft by an employee.

The narrower your practice focus is, from an industry standpoint, the easier it is to present your deep experience in it. If your firm is a general practice firm serving dozens of industries, determine whether you have eight to ten that consistently rise to the top. The more you can present your lawyers as industry experts, the better.

Caution: If you have only handled one or two matters in an industry, you are not an expert. You would not claim yourself fluent in Spanish because you are a Mexican food aficionado. If you stay on top of trends and laws in that industry, if you are a member of industry trade associations, task forces, and committees, if you speak its language—then you can position yourself as an expert.

What Will Clients Pay You For? Where Is the Money? How Should You Market and Sell the Skills You Have?

Answer the following questions:

- What can you do to get closer to your target clients?
- How do you market your practice? What tools, events, outreach, messages, and methods are the most successful?
- Do you participate in competitive pitches and "beauty contests"? How do you differentiate your firm/practice/lawyers in these competitions? What is your win rate?
- Why do clients hire your firm over another? Is it price driven?

- Who are your primary competitors by skill type or office?
- What are your goals for a new website?
- What social media tools can help you develop relationships with your target prospects? How can you exploit LinkedIn, Twitter, and Facebook to your and your prospects' benefit?
- Do traditional marketing methods work well for your skill set and practice mix? Such as writing articles or giving speeches? How are you measuring success? (You must track your success or you cannot call it "marketing.")
- Do you have an experience database that enables you to easily harness and track the expertise of your lawyers so you can easily put it in your prospect's hands?

Below are a few more questions to ask, which will help you shape your comprehensive Internet marketing plan.

Consider Your Reputation

- What do you think your reputation is? How is the firm perceived—by clients, prospects, other law firms, law students? Consider word of mouth, comments made by colleagues, client comments in awards and rankings publications, feedback on client surveys, and interviews.
- Should the perceptions they have of you change? How are they inaccurate? Be specific.
- How can your Internet marketing activities help change the perceptions and better position you?

Consider Your Culture and Style of Doing Business

Every firm culture is different. Many firms celebrate and carefully guard their culture, and are careful not to dilute it. For example, many law firms list firm values, which is their way of stating what their culture is like—it is intended to give clients and future employees a snapshot of what it is like to do business with that firm.

Shearman & Sterling LLP (www.shearman.com) includes firm values under the *About Us* global navigation tab:

Shearman & Sterling is founded on a set of values to which we have unwavering commitment:

- We **focus our utmost abilities and resources on our clients** and their interests at all times, combining high standards of professionalism with a keen understanding of their businesses so that we can help them solve any problems and surmount any challenges they may face

- We pursue **excellence** in every aspect of our professional lives, aiming to deliver quality, innovation and consistency in all aspects of our service
- We hold ourselves to high ethical standards, believing in unequivocal **integrity**
- We emphasize **teamwork** that couples effectiveness with cohesion and collegiality throughout the Firm
- We value **energy**, as individuals and as a firm, in working hard and striving to be the best in all that we undertake
- We draw upon the **diversity** of our attorneys and their talents. By collaborating with colleagues, we bring together ideas that represent various experiences, cultures and backgrounds around the globe. We bring this collective experience to bear when addressing the needs of our clients, worldwide.

We are convinced that our pursuit of these core values is fundamental to why our clients have come to rely on our services, year after year and decade after decade.

Winstead, PC (www.Winstead.com) includes its core values under *About Winstead:*

Winstead Commitment to Clients

We are more than just your attorneys—our knowledge of your business and industry makes us an extension of your core business team. We are practical, roll-up-our-sleeves lawyers committed to using our broad legal experience to relentlessly pursue innovative solutions on your terms. Our core values include:

Teamwork

We accomplish more together than we could alone, knowing that inclusiveness is essential to teamwork, and we are willing to give more than we receive.

Excellence

We expect and accept only the best.

Personal Growth

We challenge ourselves and will continually examine and raise our expectations.

Respect

We respect our clients, our adversaries and the law. We support and take pride in our firm and each other.

Integrity

We are fair and honest in all we do. The truth is absolute—regardless of consequences.

Dependability

We take responsibility, act professionally and will meet or exceed expectations.

Intensity

We are committed to and relentlessly pursue all we undertake.

Service

We serve our clients, our firm, each other, our profession and our community.

Commitment

We are loyal to our clients and each other, and provide long-term opportunity and stability.

Many firms use their culture as a badge of honor, especially when recruiting other lawyers to work there. Cultures can also be negative, however—divisive, contentious, mean-spirited, and greedy. If yours has obvious signs of negativity, a new website and social media campaign will not mask your culture problems—and creating a list of "values" will not suddenly improve how employees and others regard your firm.

Honestly answer these questions to assess whether your culture is helping you or hurting you when it comes to recruiting future clients and employees:

- How would you characterize your firm's culture and style of doing business?
- Are there negative underpinnings that negatively impact service delivery, trust among colleagues? If yes, what are they and what do you plan to do about them?
- On the positive side, what is truly unique about this firm, its clients, its lawyers?
- What adjectives would you use to describe the firm? Choose from the list below, or select adjectives of your own.

Hard-working	Trend-setting
Profitable	Fun
Creative	Smart
Growing	Big
Thoughtful	Cutting-edge
Political	Diverse
Friendly	Lifestyle-focused
Winning	Solid
Traditional	Nurturing

Competitive	International
Personal	Aggressive
Powerful	Exciting
Confident	On-the-move
Important	Innovative
Contemporary	Conservative
Relevant	Recognized by third parties

The answers to these questions will help you formulate your market position and your positioning strategy (i.e., the short "promise" that you make your visitors and clients—what they can expect when they work with you), and identify differentiating features and key messages that can set you apart in the short and long term. This information will help you choose one course of action over another and will prevent you from going to market with a "one size fits all" website and Internet marketing program. It also serves as the foundation for all design decisions.

IDENTIFY THE INTERNET TOOLS AND OPTIONS THAT MAKE THE MOST SENSE FOR YOUR FIRM

New Internet-based tools and technologies are emerging at a rapid clip. Nearly every day, there is a new "best" idea or approach to reach your audiences and connect with others. However, as stated by Chris Ducker, an Internet startup and Internet marketing consultant, "According to many sources, **more than 90% (Ninety percent) of all Internet business start-ups end in failure within the first 120 (one hundred twenty) days**. And that number is all too accurate: **NINETY PERCENT!**" The emphasis is his.

Because of the fluid nature and the fast-fail rate of many Internet marketing options, we are taking the latest look—a 2016 best practices look—at the established options, the tools that have a strong, proven stake in the ground in the legal industry and in corporate America:

- Websites and microsites
- Social media—blogs, LinkedIn, Twitter, Facebook, YouTube, plus others
- E-mail, e-alerts, and other e-mail publishing
- Multimedia—video, audio, and webinars

Selecting and committing to a few tools and channels is imperative to avoid being distracted by all the Johnny-come-latelies. Fully exploit the strengths of the tools you choose—and select them because it is where your target audiences are spending their time.

BUILDING CREDIBILITY ON THE INTERNET

Ask the question: Does our Internet-based marketing enhance our firm's reputation, relationships, and revenue? Very few firm leaders can answer an unqualified "yes." Many lawyers believe that if they show up on the Internet, they will immediately garner a following. But consider this: There are tens of millions of voices on the Internet—each hoping to be heard. How does your voice cut through the white-out blizzard of messages that your target audience receives each day?

> *The same minute of your prospect and client's time is*
> *furiously fought over not just by your competitors, but by*
> *cooking, travel, recreation, news, and adventure sites.*

The very openness and convenience that makes the Internet such a popular medium today are the very things that make credibility hard to establish. The same minute of your prospect and client's time is furiously fought over not just by your competitors, but by cooking, travel, recreation, news, and adventure sites. Your readers have to find you to know you, and they have to believe and trust you to read what you have to say.

Regardless of the particular Internet tools you use, the same basic rules apply when it comes to building credibility.

1. Choose your strategy and resulting messages and stick to them. Because you are competing with millions of self-publishers, you must be maniacal about the consistency of your messages or you will never filter through.
2. Choose the media that best match your target audiences and commit to excellent, clear communication with each webcast, podcast, or post.

    Be honest. If you bend the truth, people will find out. It takes long, hard work to establish credibility and one little falsehood will destroy it within seconds. There are numerous high profile careers that have been ruined almost overnight because of telling lies.

> *Remember, you have to answer the question in your reader's mind:*
> *Why should I care about you? Do not be afraid to share your story.*

3. Don't put just one toe in the water. This is an all-or-nothing opportunity— you will get nowhere fast if you don't commit 100 percent. For every medium you pursue, complete your "About Me" profile, include a recent photo, and briefly tell your story. Remember, you have to answer the question in your reader's mind: *Why should I care about you?* Do not be afraid to share your story.
4. Monitor and track (by setting up Google Alerts, and through Google Analytics and LinkedIn and Twitter tracking tools) who is curating and

republishing your content. It is flattering to have your posts picked up by others, whether bloggers, tweeters, or others on social media sites. But, the core messages and content of their publishing outlets might be at odds with what you are trying to promote. Avoid getting published on a site that contradicts your core principles.

5. Take the high road and stay above the fray. Loud, independent voices can turn ugly fast—do you want to be a part of a controversy that could give you an ever-lasting black eye?

6. Build a network of people you trust—and who trust you. Associating with and following smart colleagues in your field builds credibility. Be a welcome and generous participant in their Internet publishing efforts, as you wish them to be a part of yours. It is a two-way street—you have to give to get.

DETERMINE AND MAINTAIN A CONSISTENT INTERNET PERSONA

Identifying your strategy and sticking to it is the first step in establishing your Internet persona. Readers are easily fatigued—they do not have the mental bandwidth to remember more than one or two things about you. Choose your persona carefully and dedicate yourself to shaping and developing it.

So, what is an Internet persona? Fundamentally, it is a social identity that you establish in online communities, forums, and websites. For lawyers, we recommend that your persona not deviate much from who you are and the business you are in. It is often reinforced in traditional media, such as television advertising—personal injury lawyers are notable here. Many personal injury lawyers choose a hook or persona name, such as "The Texas Hammer," and all the advertising, design, and messaging reinforce that persona.

Every year, conduct a quick audit of your persona. Has it inadvertently drifted away from its original message and position? If you like where it is going, good! But review what you are publishing to ensure it is still on point.

Content Marketing

2

"Content marketing" is talked about today like it is the next big thing—put it in the kale or Brussels sprouts category. But, from the day the Internet became part of our daily lexicon, "content" has been at the center of it. The problem is that talking about it is not driving firms to embrace or invest in it. Too much law firm content is published without intention.

> *Too much law firm content is published without intention.*

For this chapter to make sense, a foundational definition is important: *Content marketing is the **business process** for distributing **valuable** content that **engages** and **acquires** a **clearly defined target audience**—with the goal of **driving revenue**.*

Some lawyers think, "I am publishing articles to my website every month. I am content marketing." No—this definition highlights that it is so much more than this.

THE RULE OF THE FIRST IMPRESSION

It is hard to get lawyers to invest the time and money in a new website or an Internet marketing campaign. They do not see new clients coming in from these tools, so they assume what they have is good enough. Here is what these lawyers do not know: According to the Corporate Executive Board (https://www.cebglobal.com), buyers go through 57 percent of the purchasing process before they speak to a sales representative, by vetting a supplier for credibility, popularity, and efficacy.

In several hundred recent interviews and focus groups with corporate buyers of legal services, they admit that this does hold true. They conduct an online search of a law firm or lawyer—starting with Google or another search engine, then go to LinkedIn to read the lawyer/firm profile. From there, if they like what they see, they will seek a link to the lawyer or firm's website. All this is done before you know the buyer is looking at you.

Then, if they like what they see, you might get a phone call or e-mail with specific queries about how you might help them. If they do not learn enough about you to act, these buyers will move on to the next lawyer on the list. And you will never be the wiser.

Strong first impressions are critical to the successful future of your business. This is a strong reason to budget for your new website or online marketing campaign.

POSITIONING STRATEGY

Positioning strategy is the basis on which a strong and effective content strategy is built. "Positioning" is the promise that you make your target audiences. Below are a few examples that, in every case, are evident on the home page of the firms' websites:

- www.keoghcox.com (Baton Rouge)—"The right ingredients for complex cases in Louisiana"
- www.minorbrown.com (Denver)—"Prepared for your 'What's Next?'"
- www.kaplankirsch.com (Denver)—"Projects that keep life moving"
- www.downeybrand.com (Sacramento)—"Advancing your interests"
- www.winstead.com (Dallas)—"Destination: Wherever you need to go"

> *Think of your positioning strategy as "a tiny little*
> *business plan boiled down into one sentence."*

As Elonide Semmes, president and founder of Right Hat, says, "Your positioning strategy may be a long sentence, but it defines your primary targets and what you are burning into their long-term memory. Think of it as a tiny little business plan boiled down into one sentence."

Leigh Dance, president of ELD International, Inc., cautions lawyers to ensure they understand how a positioning strategy translates locally in different markets. This applies not just to domestic U.S. versus international markets, but also within the United States—a local Midwest firm may choose a positioning strategy that fits its resident client base while a New York-headquartered Wall Street firm targeting banks from around the world would/should have a message that is entirely different.

YOUR FIRM VALUES WILL AFFECT AND INFORM YOUR POSITIONING STRATEGY AND CONTENT MARKETING PLANS

We spoke about firm values and culture in Chapter 1. They are not just platitudes. In a practical and important way, your values should guide your choices about what kinds of clients you serve, what you will offer them, and how you will deliver your services.

Consider these questions:

- What do we believe in?
- What do we find morally reprehensible?
- Do our firm values align with our target clients' values? (Your clients' firm values may be on their website, too—or, if not, you can ask them for a copy.)
- Are we embarrassed by our "real" values? (Is there a lot of internal infighting? Mistrust among partners? Overworking associates and staff?)
- Is our content conveying what we believe in?

Understanding your firm values is more than the five to seven bullet points on your "About Us" page on your website. It is the moral and philosophical underpinning to the content you create and publish.

Once you are intentionally aware of your own firm values, you will start to notice inconsistencies in the content published by others. For example, a firm values statement might highlight "work/life balance," but a practice description in another section of the website boasts about "24/7 availability." So, who are you really?

THE IMPORTANCE OF UNIQUE CONTENT STRATEGIES FOR EACH PRACTICE AND INDUSTRY

Since the purpose of content marketing is ultimately to drive revenue, what does that look like? What are clients hiring you to do in your signature practice and industry areas? Answer these questions:

- What are the key elements of the work you are hired to do that are revenue drivers?
- What is the most strategic and distinguishing part of that work?

- What is in the news today about your signature practice and industry areas?
- What do you have to say about what is in the news? This could be a content marketing opportunity.
- How can you make your point of view memorable and unique? Read and listen to what others are publishing about what is in the news—what can you say to make you stand out and get noticed?
- Will influential people (those who either buy your services or influence those who do) read your posts or listen to your podcasts/webcasts and follow you?

It is difficult for "full-service" law firms to choose their most distinguishing areas of practice, because all practices want to participate. Or, if not participate, they at least want the same attention that others are getting—it is politically charged.

You will never get anywhere if you are guided only by your law firm's rules of political correctness. Even the largest full service firms do not have the resources to devote to every practice area to ensure they are an active voice on social media. They must pick and choose, and here is what they consider:

- What are the hottest topics in the news that align with our key practice and industry areas?
- How long do we think each topic will be in the headlines?
- What lawyers are eager to participate—and are committed for the long term?

Once you have defined your signature areas (this is what emerges from answering both sets of questions above), invest in those first. Say mergers and acquisitions (M&A) is one of your signature areas and you want to start an M&A blog for your group. These are preliminary questions to ask:

- What are the key elements of our M&A work that are the top revenue drivers?
- What is the most strategic and distinguishing part of our M&A work? Is it the industries we serve? Is it the size of the deal? Is it the arcane issues we are covering?
- What is in today's business news about M&A? What is spreading on social media and by the major news outlets? What are analysts, other lawyers, and bankers saying about the M&A trends?
- What do you have to say about the M&A trends that you see and others are covering? How can you make your point of view memorable so you have a chance of slicing through all the other commentary and being heard?

If you have identified five signature practice areas for your firm,
each one needs its own content strategy because the buyers for each
area are different. Their motivations and needs are different.

Your content strategy for your M&A practice will be different than it would be for your intellectual property, hospitality, or real estate practices. If you have identified five signature areas for your firm, each one needs its own content strategy because the buyers for each area are different. Their motivations and needs are different. What works for M&A may not work for intellectual property. Your over-arching goal for any content strategy should be to build trust with your audience. The key is learning how to do that.

Here is how *not* to build trust—only write about yourselves. This is the equivalent of holding up a mirror and preening—people ignore these messages, and they have the opposite effect on trust. Plus, too many of these messages waste a visitor's time.

Focus on your audiences and what *they* need and want.

Eric Fletcher, the chief marketing officer at Liskow & Lewis, co-authored a book with Kent Huffman called *8 Mandates for Social Media Marketing Success*. His chapter, "Mandate 8—Continue Listening," has a paragraph entitled "Where Marketing Goes Awry," which starts, "Here's the problem: we believe that once we've delivered a message—written it, posted it on a fan page, recorded it, spoken it aloud, hit 'send,' or organized it into a PowerPoint—that we have communicated." But, have you?

According to Fletcher, not really. Because we are not listening. At the point I hit the "send" button, all I have done is talk. It is almost too elementary to answer the question in this book, "How do we learn to listen?" But, we are going to do it anyway. Listening really means two things:

1. It means reading/listening to what others are saying about topics, people, companies, and causes that are important to you (and your clients). It means following them in various social media and "hearing" their points of view.
2. And, in the social media context, "listening," which is also known as social media monitoring, is the process of identifying and assessing what is being said about a company, individual, product, or brand on the Internet.

There are several free listening tools that you can set up, including Google Alerts, Hootsuite and TweetDeck, Icerocket, Social Mention, and Topsy.

WHERE DOES YOUR CONTENT END UP? HOW DO PEOPLE FIND IT? DESIGN A 360-DEGREE CONTENT STRATEGY

In today's world of seemingly countless communication channels, it is helpful to determine which channels make the most sense for your firm, its signature practices, and the particular strengths of your lawyers. What are the best channels to consider?

The 360-degree range of options you have and all that you can leverage

Study this *360-Degree Content Strategy* infographic designed by author Deborah McMurray's company, Content Pilot LLC. This displays the range of options from and to which you can syndicate and leverage content from various online and offline communication vehicles. Think of the channels listed here as your distribution network. Not every one of your signature practice areas will utilize every channel you see here—the channels and media you exploit depend on the buyers for those particular services, and how they spend their time, how they make decisions, and what they read/listen to. This book is focusing entirely on Internet marketing opportunities.

WHAT INTERNET MARKETING TOOLS ARE THE BEST FIT FOR YOUR FIRM, YOUR PRACTICE MIX, AND LAWYERS?

Website

Does every law firm need a website? Yes. In this world where most humans own at least two hand-held devices, and they walk (and drive!) looking down at them, it would be nearly impossible to be noticed without some kind of effective online presence. Given that your firm is being evaluated online before you even know it, as described in "The Rule of the First Impression" above, it is standard operating procedure for successful and growing law firms.

Lawyers can establish a simple, but clear and differentiating, website on a shoestring, or they can spend hundreds of thousands—or more than a million—dollars. Either budget can be successful as long as you know your audience, and are focused on the fundamentals of good positioning and communication described earlier in this book.

Social Media—And How It Has Been Affected by Mobile Devices

"Social media" is the umbrella term we use for blogs, Twitter, LinkedIn, Facebook, YouTube, Instagram, Wikipedia, and other websites where individuals generate their own content and self-publish. We are at the tip of the iceberg, as the size and scope of the technologies, platforms, tools, and modes of producing content continue to grow exponentially.

> *This mobile shift is not our imagination, it is clearly documented. We know and can watch the consumption behaviors of our audiences.*

The surge in our use of mobile devices has caused a cataclysmic shift in how buyers of legal services and others are consuming social media and other content. Accessing their smartphones over lunch or happy hour and reaching for their tablets at night after dinner is all tracked by Google Analytics and other programs—this mobile shift is not our imagination, it is clearly documented. We know and can watch the consumption behaviors of our audiences.

Note: Buyers of legal services know we are tracking them, so they have an expectation that our content choices and delivery will be smarter and more tailored to what they need over time.

Where are *your* target buyers reading content? Whom do they follow? What subject matter will always get their attention? Because there are literally billions of content pieces available on the Internet for feasting, what can you do to attract a following for your content that can develop relationships, build reputation, and ultimately drive revenue?

How do you find out? Well, as simple as this sounds, ask your most important clients whom they follow and what they like. Short of asking, you can see whom they follow on Twitter and to whom they are connected on LinkedIn. You can track what they like just by doing a little investigating and a lot of listening.

Remember the two definitions of "listening" earlier in this chapter—Eric Fletcher writes, "Any effort to develop an effective social media marketing strategy is built on a listening foundation or platform . . . One of the great challenges . . . is to resist the temptation to bypass the process of laying the foundation [for communication] and jump straight to the sales proposition." He continues, "effective listening will define the fabric and dimension of effective messaging."

Your investment in social media tools and campaigns should align directly with the needs and desires of your clients and prospects. Establish your footing where they are spending their time.

Video and Audio—Critical Content Tools

Video and audio (podcasts) are proven boosters of relationships and reputation on a law firm's website. The analytics prove it. One American Lawyer (AmLaw) 200 firm, which has made a concerted effort to drive visitors to and keep traffic on its website through video and podcasts, has nearly tripled the time spent by visitors on the website, and more than doubled the number of pages they visit.

A rule of thumb is that shorter videos are viewed more frequently than long ones—you can create a video or podcast of substance and still have it be five minutes or less.

> *A rule of thumb is that shorter videos are viewed*
> *more frequently than long ones.*

Many lawyers are quick to dismiss video because of what they have seen on YouTube and other social media sites (no more cats playing the piano, please!). The fact is that YouTube (owned by Google) is the second largest search engine in the world, and having thoughtful, relevant videos on it will boost your search engine optimization—and thus, the traffic to your website.

With a handful of exceptions, the videos prepared by too many law firms show lawyers as a "talking head," speaking about a development in the law, lawyers talking about firm culture, or firm leaders talking about their commitment to diversity, their communities, or how nice their people are. The production value ranges from quite terrible to pretty good—but they are mostly not compelling and not differentiating. Most of the lawyers—even those with the best and enthusiastic intentions—come across as boring and dry. And the videos are always too long.

Adam Stock, the director of marketing and business development at Allen Matkins, was an early adopter—as was his law firm—of video on www.allenmatkins .com. His rule is: "None of our videos show attorneys speaking into the camera— no talking heads." Note that we cover more of what Allen Matkins is doing, as well as other examples, in greater detail in Chapter 13.

How does one find the time to script and shoot one video, let alone dozens? The secret is leveraging your content—doing video versions of communications that you are already creating/writing, material that you are already publishing. Stock states that they create four categories of videos:

1. Centered around a legal alert announcing a change in regulation or law (they do written and video alerts)
2. Business tips and insight (frequently appearing in print on a blog)
3. Press releases (also found in print on the Allen Matkins website)
4. The firm's involvement in their communities (also noted on the firm's website and on Allen Matkins community blog).

Generally, he continues, "We focus on information that you didn't know you needed to know." Stock believes that the connection between a lawyer and a buyer of legal services can happen so much faster in video—in video done right. Visitors to your website get a visual/audio preview of what it is like to do business with you.

The advantages are enormous—for both your firm and your visitors—your visitors get to choose when, how, and where they consume a video, podcast, or webinar. You may be reaching your most important clients while you are sleeping or when they are in the gym.

E-mail

We discuss e-mail marketing in great detail in Chapter 12, but we mention it here because it is still one of the most popular vehicles used in content marketing. It is popular particularly for the quick dissemination of an alert or commentary about a late-breaking topic. Most law firms of any size publish alerts by practice, industry, and subject matter, with frequency that depends on the length of the news cycle.

Unfortunately, because of research, approvals, rounds of revisions, etc., the law firm "alerts" are often reporting on yesterday's news. And the targeted, plum recipient has received six or more "alerts" discussing the same issues. *Caution*: Do not jump into it if your processes cannot support immediate distribution. And, if you are committed to it, reconfigure your process so that you can be first—or close—to disseminate it.

For years, marketers have debated about the optimal length of an e-mail subject line, with some believing short and concise gets higher readability, and others insisting that longer subject lines drive better consumption. George Bilbrey, the president of Return Path and frequent contributor to MediaPost's Email Insider blog, wrote "We recently sifted through more than eighteen million subject lines sent to more than two million subscribers to find out whether subscribers' actual read rates pointed to an optimal length. We found none: the sweet spot remains elusive. In fact, at least in this sample, it didn't exist—not mathematically, anyway."

He pointed out, however, that 100-character or longer subject lines were the worst-read of all the line lengths.

Caution: Know where people are reading your e-mails—desktop, tablet, or phone—if you use a current e-mail program such as those discussed in Chapter 12, they can track the devices where your visitors are opening the e-mail. If on a phone, long subject lines will be truncated, so avoid them. And ensure that they are descriptive—tell your readers enough so they will feel compelled to read on.

Webinars and Other Educational Programming

Webinars have improved considerably since the last edition of this book (published in 2007), primarily because the providers are better and are offering better tools. Like video or podcasts, webinars are scheduled and presented, but visitors to your website who missed the original air date can view it at their convenience if you archive it. Note that we also discuss webinars in greater detail in Chapter 13.

How can you produce a webinar that people will want to watch?

Lawyers and marketers jump on the webinar bandwagon without answering this question: Will it be useful and important to our audience? Also ask this: Do we have something to say that is better and different than what others will say on this topic? For each slide you create, question whether it is truly adding value to your message. Some topics are better suited to the webinar format than others. Consider the following:

- A detailed look at a topic from a fresh angle—a new angle can make an old topic hot again.
- A panel discussion of a timely issue in a changing industry, such as energy or healthcare. Invite other experts to join you as moderator/host.
- A "how-to" tutorial about contract or employment law, for example.

Look for ways to leverage a presentation from a conference speaking engagement and adapt it as a webinar. Remember, using the 360-Degree Content Strategy infographic as your guide, seek ways to leverage past work and syndicate your content.

Two things will ruin a webinar experience—poor content and bad technology. Rehearsals with your technology are imperative—the webinar platforms are not always intuitive and, unless you own them, they may be unfamiliar. In addition to learning the webinar technology, ensure that you use a cell phone with a headset or use a landline with a headset. Most computers have microphones, but they are not always trustworthy, and they can sound tinny and garbled when recorded. We do not recommend using the computer microphone for your webinar.

Your content consists of two elements: your slide deck and your script. They are not the same thing. Avoid reading your slide deck (your visitors can do that themselves). Rather, take highlights from your script and call them out on the screen. Your script is the story you are telling—it is your map and GPS—it will keep you focused and help you avoid distractions and unintended rabbit trails. Your slide deck should be an attractive mix of compelling images (avoid clip art), even video clips, and legible words and phrases that punctuate and add color to the story you are telling.

AWARDS, RANKINGS, AND DIRECTORY LISTINGS

Lawyers assume that buyers of legal services pay attention to and, in fact, make hiring decisions based on the awards and rankings that they have won. In client interviews over the past decade with business-to-business buyers, nearly all said they do not consider these rankings in any hiring decision. Many do not notice the press releases that announce the awards at all, because they are not on those pages of the website. For smaller and more local law firms, they might be helpful referral sources.

Having said this, they are important to the lawyers and firms, and show distinction in certain areas of the law. It is highly time consuming for the marketing/business development team to unearth relevant matters to report and complete the applications for up to 1,000 (for very large firms) different ranking organizations and directories. Before you invest this time and money, be clear and realistic about what you hope to get from it.

Certain practice areas have their own ranking organizations and criteria, such as insurance law and *Best's Directory of Recommended Insurance Attorneys and Adjusters*. Thomson Reuters publishes its well-established League Tables quarterly, which include deal data in the following areas: M&A, equity, debt, syndicated loans, municipals, project finance, joint ventures, and debt restructuring. Bloomberg publishes M&A Advisory data that covers activity and advisors in nine countries.

Conducting interviews with buyers of legal services, Chambers USA Directory covers numerous areas of law by state, while its parent, Chambers and Partners, ranks firms and practitioners in other parts of the world. These are coveted rankings, because, according to Chambers, qualities on which rankings are assessed include: technical legal ability, professional conduct, client service, commercial awareness/astuteness, diligence, commitment, plus others.

Other lawyer-popular ranking organizations include The Best Lawyers in America and Super Lawyers (www.superlawyers.com). For Super Lawyers, lawyers enter the candidate pool by being formally nominated by a peer or if identified by the research department during the research process. For Best Lawyers, inclusion is based entirely on peer-review by leading lawyers about the professional abilities of their colleagues within the same geographical area and legal practice area.

All of these organizations have websites; if you are included, ensure that your listing is as robust and informative as possible, and that it is 100 percent accurate. Link from your website bio to your pages on these rankings sites. Include the "badges" for each award on your biography, but be sensible about this—if you have ten awards, do not include ten badges. It looks like you are more focused on your awards than you are on your clients' legal problems and concerns.

Today's Websites

3

THE BIG PICTURE

As mentioned in Chapter 2, a law firm can spend very little money for a basic website, or a million dollars or more on a website filled with features and functionality that serve multiple and specific target audiences. The right answer to the question *"How much should I spend?"*—is *"What do you want to achieve?"* and *"What clients do you hope to serve?"* Don't under-spend, but do not over-spend, either. This is your most important and public marketing and business development tool—do it right.

Most law firm websites are average. Or worse. Herein lies the opportunity—be thoughtful and diligent about improving yours. Take considered chances.

In her interviews with buyers of legal services, Content Pilot's Deborah McMurray learned that they were unhappy, unfazed, and unimpressed with the law firm websites that they visited. As a result, in 2005, McMurray designed the first criteria to analyze these sites—*Ten Foundational Best Practices for Law Firm Websites*—after she analyzed visitor behavior on law firm websites by tracking analytics, studying broad web industry trends and best practices, reviewing what buyers were seeking, and learning what technologies and tools were available at the time. Her then-consultancy sponsored a research study of the American Lawyer (AmLaw) 100 websites (the 100 largest firms headquartered in the United States), based on the Ten Foundational Best Practices and several attributes that fall under each one.

The first AmLaw 100 study using the Ten Foundational Best Practices was done in 2005. Content Pilot LLC continued the research in 2006, 2007, 2010, and 2013, adjusting the Ten Foundational Best Practices and related attributes each year as visitor needs, technology, and buyer expectations changed.

The most recent Content Pilot study ("How Do They Measure Up? 2016 AmLaw Global 50 Websites: Ten Foundational Best Practices") was completed in August 2016, with a comprehensive White Paper of Trends and Insights, as well as results, published in November 2016. It is available free for download at http://www.content pilot.com/subscribe.

This research substantiates the claims that law firm clients made in 2005—and still make today—that even the largest firm websites are *average*, because that is literally how they scored. In the 2016 study, 50 law firms were analyzed and more than half of them—26 firms—ranked "Fair" (a range of 51–70 on a 100-point scale). This means that visitors, in many cases, will not be satisfied and they will not rely on these sites as an important and valuable resource. Chapter 5 is focused entirely on the Ten Foundational Best Practices, which are easily adapted to law firms of any size—small or large.

What is the big picture reason to have a website? Too many law firms are *not* focused on client communication first—they are too focused on internal messages about their awards, practice areas (all sounding of equal weight and strength because of the political concerns noted in Chapter 2 about featuring one over others), and new lawyers that they want to advertise. Do buyers of legal services care about these things—awards and such? Do they view them as just "nice," or do they move the needle in their decision-making about whether to hire you? You better find out before you launch your new site.

THE VISITOR EXPERIENCE

Understand the demographics and ethnographics of your target buyers of legal services. Of course, understand *all* your audiences—law school recruits, laterals, staff, as well—but most firms want to design their sites first to attract and keep prospects and clients. Given limited resources (time and money), law firms typically design the site to appeal to the lawyers in the firm—and people like them, believing if the lawyers are happy, the clients will like it. That may or may not be true, especially if your clients span many generations, titles, geographies, job responsibilities, and priorities.

This is why too many of today's websites are firm and lawyer-focused, not client-focused. It is more difficult to plan and design a site that can accommodate multigenerational, multicultural, and language differences.

Challenge yourself to analyze your current client base and the profile of prospects you hope to represent one day. To figure this out, large firms often hire professional market researchers and spend well into the six-figures on first party research. Others who do not have a hefty research budget sift through third-party research that is available in databases and on the Internet. Whatever your budget, set aside the time and money to interview current clients about how they use the Internet in their jobs, and how they use law firm and other websites. (While you have them on the phone, conduct a client loyalty and satisfaction interview at the same time. Such interviews tackle assumptions about how the firm is doing and how pleased the clients are, and it presents a golden opportunity for a better functioning, more intimate relationship.)

In a recent Networked Insights study, "Millennials: Empowerment vs Anxiety," which analyzed more than 18,000 consumer conversations across social media for two months, researchers found that, for millennials, *emotions* are critically important to their buying decisions in certain categories—technology, automobiles, travel, and finance. For this study, millennials covered the ages 20 to 35, and, depending on the services you offer, the industries you target, and clients you want to serve, this age group may cover a large segment that is critical to your success.

The study found they make purchases that are largely based on eliminating anxiety or increasing their empowerment. Understanding these emotional drivers is key for all brands to successfully connect with them—including law firm brands. Lawyers may dismiss this by saying that purchasing legal services is *different*—it is more *intellectual*. Even with the most arcane of niche practice areas and with the largest of budgets, buyers of legal services are still choosing a firm or lawyer based on emotion. When they are crafting their short list of firms and lawyers to consider, they *are* making an intellectual decision—evaluating technical expertise, experience, fees, geographic reach, and so on. But when they are selecting the one firm to hire, it shifts—and they are asking, "Do I trust this person? Do I like her? Would I enjoy having a beer with him?"

According to Networked Insights President and Chief Operating Officer Gerry Komlofske, millennials "are the first generation to grow up with the true power of the Internet." Thus, they are used to "being able to get information from others in an anonymous way. . . . And they are now at a time when they are buying autos, houses, having babies, looking for insurance."

And they are having social media conversations about those things. Because this is how they are living their lives, it means they will seek professional advice the same way—physicians, accountants, insurance brokers, and lawyers.

So, what does this mean? It means that millennials are the future of your practice, if not a major presence today. It means that your website visitor experience (and the experience you offer in social media) must not strictly be "just the facts, ma'am." If buyers of all ages respond to emotion, law firms must find a way to engage with them in a meaningful way.

Every client hires lawyers because they have an opportunity (empowerment) or they have a problem (anxiety). Baby boomer and generation X buyers operate the same way as millennials. The difference is they historically haven't relied on the Internet to find the answers, reviews, and other clients' opinions. The prevalence of this is increasing, however; it is verified in another research study conducted by ALM Legal Intelligence, the Zeughauser Group, and Green Target about corporate counsel's use of social media as an influencer in their hiring of outside counsel. Titled "2014 State of Digital & Content Marketing Survey," and released in May 2014, it identified the use of social media platforms by corporate counsel buyers of legal services. It confirmed that since the first survey was conducted in 2010, buyers of all age groups are increasingly relying on blogs, LinkedIn, Twitter, and Facebook to obtain information about relevant subjects that affect their companies and work. They are using these tools to inform their buying decisions.

Norm Rubenstein, a partner with the Zeughauser Group, who was very involved with designing the research and publishing the white papers, said the following:

> Several years of GreenTarget/Zeughauser Group surveys consistently have shown that the focus and brevity of digital communication tools, such as blogs, accommodate the information needs of a wide range of in-house decision makers. Blogs tend to be specific and searchable, so instead of lengthy newsletters that arrive as PDFs and get filed or printed for another day, a relevant blog post is consumable in real time. And progressive firms that use Twitter or LinkedIn to highlight the existence of these blog posts or other thought leadership materials of interest serve to increase the number of people who become aware of their existence. The added benefit to a multi-pronged social media strategy is that now focused thought leadership is driving traffic to law firm websites. This gives the thoughtful presentation of positioning strategy and differentiated approaches to service-delivery the chance for a qualified, interested audience, which might never have come to the site at all.

Visitor Experience on the Go

It is more difficult today to manage your visitors' experience with your website. Are they on a train or plane viewing your site on an iPad mini, an older, larger tablet, a Samsung Android phone, a smaller, older Apple iPhone, or a larger 6s+? Perhaps they are on a laptop with a screen size that could be 12 inches to 17 inches. Or, are they in their offices with huge desktop monitors? Every visitor, regardless of device, has an expectation that you will deliver a perfect experience—meaning, they can navigate easily and quickly find what they are seeking, regardless of the device that is serving it up.

Fortunately, Google Analytics and other measurement tools show the devices visitors are using, the pages they are visiting, and how long they are staying. There is no guesswork here.

Jakob Nielsen and Don Norman of Nielsen Norman Group (www.nngroup.com), the godfathers of usability since the birth of websites as we know them, define user experience like this:

> The first requirement for an exemplary user experience is to meet the exact needs of the customer, without fuss or bother. Next comes simplicity and elegance that produce products that are a joy to own, a joy to use. True user experience goes far beyond giving customers what they say they want, or providing checklist features.

In order to achieve high-quality user experience in a company's offerings there must be a seamless merging of the services of multiple disciplines, including engineering, marketing, graphical and industrial design, and interface design.

How do you design a site that pleases everyone? Keep reading.

Your Audience: Are Your Visitors Global or Local?

Most law firm leaders know the make-up of their top 100 clients, and whether they are U.S. headquartered with operations around the country, a conglomerate with operations around the globe, a domestic manufacturing company, a startup software enterprise, or individuals who need estate plans, divorces, custody battle resolution, or damage recovery from a personal injury. Google Analytics also shows from what country, region, state, and neighborhood your website visitors are coming.

E. Leigh Dance, president of ELD International, a leading international consultancy that works with law firms and corporate legal departments, offers a checklist to help firms better understand their clients and their needs. Her over-arching advice is to "[m]ake sure your content aligns with a multi-dimensional understanding of your clients." Here is Leigh's checklist—your client analysis can break down like this:

- General: all firm clients
- Clients in core practices and industry groups
- Clients in certain places: urban/rural, west coast/east coast, emerging/ mature, Chinese/Latin American
- Clients in varying roles: legal, compliance, business heads, boards, finance/audit, shareholders
- Your clients' customers: who are *their* customers?
- Clients with different priorities: do they want to grow, save money, save time, reduce risk, win battles . . .?

Dance continues, with advice for business-to-business law firms that have offices outside the United States:

> For firms with international clients, question the assumption that English is the language of global business. A minority of your business clients worldwide are proficient in English. Outside the United States, few use the term "attorney." Lawyers are called lawyers, or in former English colony countries like the Emirates and South Africa, they're usually called solicitors. You cannot fully understand your clients without talking to your local lawyers (and preferably your clients) at the source, which can be complicated for firms with offices in many countries.
>
> Understand who else your clients buy from in each market and why. Without that information, your content could be just like that of your competitors down the street.
>
> Finally, figure out what you can afford to do, and what you have time to do— it's essential to planning your content strategy. You simply can't cover everything your firm does, and if you try, you'll fail, because your efforts will be superficial.

You absolutely must be selective and focused—and educate your firm leadership about how this focus pays off.

Elonide Semmes, president of Right Hat, a research and design firm that serves several industries, including legal, says there are several design and other considerations when your audience is international:

- Images—Be careful with copy embedded on images since it will not translate automatically. Also be careful with your alt tags, which provide alternative text when images cannot be displayed.
- Color—Be aware of international color connotations.
- Domains—Consider multiple domains for international search engine optimization (SEO) benefit.
- Wording—Avoid slang, list the country on upcoming events, and always hire a professional translator.
- Fonts—Be sure the fonts you choose for text and headers will display in various languages.

All this ties into creating a comfortable and effective visitor experience. If they feel at home on your website, they will come back, and they are more likely to refer your firm to others.

Where Do You Begin?

Semmes, with hundreds of client interviews behind her, says, "If you aren't sure where to begin—in terms of understanding your clients—begin here: Ask your clients 'Where do we as a firm add the highest value to your company?' From that single question, we almost always get the nuances of where a firm should spend more time."

In summary, to create the best experience for the maximum number of visitors, you must:

- Know and understand your audience (local, global, and so on)
- Be clear about your own strengths and where you are a market or practice leader or a niche player (you cannot effectively be something to everyone)
- Understand your competitors, whom they represent, and what they are saying
- Own your firm strategy, a differentiating positioning strategy, and the key messages that support both
- Analyze the devices your visitors are using to access your site, the pages they visit, the bounce rate, and where they enter and exit

- Write, produce, and publish content that is relevant to your top clients and targets, and that reinforces your practice and industry strengths and your lawyers as thought-leaders
- Design an attractive website with intuitive navigation and search features, where visitors can easily find what they need
- Ensure that your graphic design adapts to all or most screen sizes, without compromising the quality and integrity of your design and brand.

Planning and Designing Your Website

4

The most common questions law firms ask about websites are:

1. How long does it take?
2. How much will it cost?
3. How long will it last?

Lawyers, marketers, and administrators often ask how long a website project should take from start to launch. As with many questions, the answer is "it depends," but on average, a smaller site can take three to six months, and a large site, six to 12 months, or longer.

> *How long does it take to plan and build? On average, a smaller site can take three to six months, and a large site, six to 12 months, or longer.*

The answer about cost is also "it depends" (of course). A basic open source platform site done by a freelance developer could cost $5,000 or less. An enterprise site that starts with strategy, built on a sophisticated content management system (CMS) with features and functionality that boost engagement, all packaged within a differentiating design—can cost several hundred thousand dollars on up.

HOW MUCH WILL IT COST?

There are numerous variables that will drive cost:

- *Designing a clear and differentiating positioning strategy*—Many vendors are not skilled in this area and do not offer it. But some do, and it will serve as the "theme" for your firm and website as long as it is live. Strategy is a critical component that drives important choices and decisions during the planning and design phases. It also is the foundation for feature and functionality selections.
- *Advanced search features*—There are several popular search features that most of us are familiar with today. Did you mean? (Google uses this), predictive search (think Google searches), and featuring/tagging "popular" terms all add to the visitor experience, ensuring that visitors *find* what they are seeking.
- *Multimedia management*—Video and podcast hosting consumes site bandwidth, causing it to respond slowly. If you plan to include several videos and podcasts, it is best to have a media manager tool (often offered as a special module on content management systems) and also to engage a separate hosting provider, such as Brightcove or Libsyn, from the main website.
- *New lawyer photos*—It is always recommended to shoot new photos when you do a major redesign. Nothing says "I am uncomfortable with who I am today" like a lawyer who has aged 20 years or put on 50 pounds since the last photo shoot. When a prospect visits the website bio, then meets the lawyer for the first time, the prospect will not recognize the lawyer—and this is an instant, unspoken breach of trust. Shoot new photos with every new hairstyle or color, pair of glasses, Lasik surgery, and weight gain or loss.

> *Shoot new photos with every new hairstyle or color, pair of glasses, Lasik surgery, and weight gain or loss.*

- *Mobile devices*—Your website must perform well on all mobile devices. This involves designing a separate mobile site for smartphones, or employing responsive web design (RWD) with at least one breakpoint, but probably two or three. Each breakpoint costs more, but it ensures that the visitor experiences on a large tablet, a mini tablet, a large iPhone or Android, or smaller smartphones are consistent and equally good. We discuss RWD and breakpoints later in Chapter 5.
- *Content*—If you can fit it into your budget, hire an experienced copywriter who is used to working with lawyers. Write at least new biographies for every lawyer, all following the same format, and new practice and industry descriptions. Include new home page strategy copy that reinforces your positioning strategy and identifies your brand promise, as well as new

copy for top-level landing pages—About the firm, Careers, News/Events, Offices, and others.

- *Beautiful design*—This involves having courage. Resist the temptation to follow the law firm crowd and, instead, embrace the "these don't look like a law firm" designs. Usually, great design costs more than bad design (not always, though). Avoid cookie cutter offerings and companies that only sell certain "templates." Spend the money on design that is created just for your firm. Designing for your clients' satisfaction and happiness, not your lawyers', is the key. You can see examples in our design discussion in Chapter 5.

- *Integration and feeds*—Feeding in blog and Twitter posts—as recommended in this book, integration with Cvent (www.cvent.com) or other event management software, and other social media integration can drive cost. Many firm marketing teams want to save steps, so when they post a new alert or update, or publish details about a new event on the website, they want those posts to automatically create posts on Twitter, LinkedIn, and Facebook. Leveraging time and effort this way also ensures that the details are accurate when they are "syndicated."

- *Unique page organization*—Many firms prefer the use of tabs on bios and practice pages, which keeps a visitor "above the fold" as much as possible. You can see examples later in Chapter 5. Having flexibility in the tab names from lawyer to lawyer or practice to practice is popular—lawyers can choose the tab titles that best match their practice and business development style.

- *Stock and original photography (or illustration)*—And the time it takes to find it or shoot it. Photography and illustration can make or break a website. Avoid clip art and trite photos that say "law firm." Instead, a fine designer will recommend photo or illustration styles that will further your strategic messaging and add impact to the visitor experience. Expect to pay your designer for "image research," which is often billed hourly—outside of the quoted design cost, as well as the cost of all photos or illustrations you use on your website. Some designers also add a surcharge on top of the cost of the images you are buying. This can range from 20–100 percent the cost of the image. This may be in addition to the hourly fee, or in lieu of it.

- *A state of the art CMS*—Because content is king, and no visitors come to your website other than to view your content, it must be easy to keep current. The best websites today are those that are 100 percent (or close to that) content managed, meaning the law firm handles all the content updates, not the vendor. These are sophisticated tools, designed for ease of use by non-technical people, such as marketers, administrators, some administrative assistants or secretaries, even lawyers.

- *Search engine optimization (SEO) and search engine marketing*—If you launch a new site, you want your content to be optimized, so it is easy to find on the major search engines. Some CMSs enable owners to manage

SEO on a page-by-page basis. This feature typically comes with the CMS purchase. There are numerous consultants—and some charlatans—who offer SEO services, some making bold promises about what they can "guarantee" you in search rankings. Do not believe any of that hogwash, but there are fine consultants who legitimately can help you think through the best ways to get found. For a much deeper discussion about SEO, please read Chapter 14.

- *Content migration*—Someone has to load your content, often pulling much of it from your current website and loading the new practice, industry, and bio pages. Many vendors do not offer this service, and it is critical to have your content loaded, cross-linked, and tested before launch. Some of it can be digitally migrated by mapping the fields from your old site to the new one, but often it takes a human to eyeball things and ensure each page looks right.

- *Project management*—Every website budget includes a certain number of hours for project management, but particular clients need more hand-holding, decisions take longer (thus extending the timeline), and scope changes in features and functionality require additional time to manage and test the features. Your project manager is your best friend during planning, design, and development, but remember that every hour you require counts against the time the manager has allotted. Discuss your working style with your website vendor—if you think you will want more time than would typically be included, ask for a change order that will cover the extra time that you require.

AN OUTLINE OF THE TYPICAL PHASES OF YOUR WEBSITE

1. *Statement of work and scope of work (SOW) discussion*—This is defined in detail in Chapter 7, but briefly, the SOW outlines every aspect of the website engagement and what you should expect to receive. This is often determined and finalized during the negotiation and contract phase. Your vendor may recommend that certain SOW features move to a post-launch phase two, if you have a drop-dead deadline for launch that cannot shift to accommodate all the features you want.

2. *Strategy*—A critical foundation of your website project. Too many firms leave this out (see the first of the Ten Foundational Best Practices, "Communicating Your Message," in Chapter 5).

3. *Site architecture, wireframes, and functional requirements*—If you do not know what a wireframe is, think of it as you would the architectural drawings for your house—but these are for your website. Site architecture is a related document that includes descriptions and diagrams of all the functionality

and features on your website. Developers use site architecture typically, and designers use the wireframes from start to launch. These are important documents that firmly lock in the scope of your project and its budget.

4. *Graphic design*—Your designer will produce an agreed-upon number of unique page designs or templates (this term is frequently used in the design world—but do not confuse this use with the earlier discussion related to "cookie cutter" templates), typically the home page, bio landing page and details page, practice/industry landing and details page, news/events landing and details page, search and search results, and careers landing and one or more details pages. About the firm and other pages may follow the same format as any one of the pages mentioned here. As you add new unique page designs, cost will go up.

5. *Design consistency review*—This is where your designer scours the website during alpha testing for inconsistencies, ensuring that everything appears as it should. Many vendors eliminate this critical step, trusting they got it right. This rigor is critical to ensuring that your visitors have a consistent experience one page to the next. And, frankly, it ensures that you are getting the design that you paid for.

6. *Programming*—Depending on the complexity of your site, this often takes two or more months. It can take up to four or five months, or even longer—again, depending on features and functionality.

7. *Content migration*—This is typically done after the CMS/website administration tool is completed and ready for use. As noted above, certain content can be migrated in by mapping fields from your current site to your new site. The remaining content will be entered by hand by your vendor team and/or your employees.

8. *Testing*—Alpha testing is where the vendor team cleans up issues, nitpicks the design and ensures it looks like the approved documents, and tests the features and functionality. Beta testing (sometimes called user acceptance testing, or UAT) is when the site is released to the law firm for two or more weeks for its testing, final content changes, issue fixes, and preparation for launch. This is *not* the time to change the website—avoid design, feature, and functionality changes. Focus on issues and content only. If you missed something during planning and design and it must be completed or added before launch, expect a time delay and SOW enhancement—a price increase based on the number of hours (time and materials) required.

9. *Launch*—Your site should be locked down (meaning you cannot access it) for two days prior to launch, to enable your developers to make final adjustments. Your vendor project manager and developer will work with your information technology director or employee to arrange the Domain Name System (DNS) change from your current site to the new site. Once the "launch button is pushed," it can take up to 24 hours for your site to

be seen across the country. Certain geographies may see it right away—others may take hours.

DNS is like calling 411 for a phone number. When people want to go to your website (xyzlawfirm.com) their computers will get your address from DNS. So when you change your domain or DNS, you are updating the address people will use to get to your new site. This is seamless to your visitors—it is all under the hood. Technically, your domain name is not the same as your URL. Your domain name is xyzlawfirm.com, but the URL includes other information that directs visitors to specific pages of your site, such as http://www.xyzlawfirm.com/people/johnasmith. (More on domain names below.)

AND THE FINAL QUESTION: HOW LONG WILL IT LAST?

Expect to live with and support your new site for four to five years. You may want a home page refresh before then; or you can design your site where you have the ability to change images and content on your home page without requiring your vendor's assistance. Some design vendors say three years is long enough. Because these projects are expensive and time-consuming, many firms are fatigued by them—and they do not want to start planning again for four or more years. If your strategy is smart and differentiating, your design and imagery elevating, and your vendor's technology stays current, your site should weather well.

It is imperative, however, to keep your content very fresh. For you to get your money's worth, your content should be updated *frequently*. Schedule content updates—home page every two to four weeks; bios every six months; practice and industry pages every year; experience/matter updates should occur all the time—as they happen.

DOMAIN NAMES

In the early days of law firm websites, firms abbreviated the firm name. For example, Hanson Johnson Thompson and Swanson LLP became www.hjts.com or hjtslaw.com and Pony Smith Thatcher LLP became www.pstlawfirm.com. Today, visitors (especially law students) search intuitively—we type in "hansonjohnson" and "ponysmith" and hope the firms' websites will appear. Your domain name is an important part of your firm's positioning and branding (learn more about branding under "Design" in Chapter 5) strategy—it should advance your firm's name in the marketplace. Initials do not do that, except sometimes for the very largest firms. For example, Latham & Watkins' domain is www.lw.com—a firm of that size and stature can get by with using initials. For most firms, it is recommended that you use your actual firm name.

Try to rise above the politics and egos and choose a sensible, short domain name that is intuitive to find.

For small firms with several partner names included in the firm name, shortening the domain name can be a political hot potato. It is best to use the "street name" (what people actually call you), but that is often shorter than the string of names included in the actual firm legal name. This is what often motivates law firm partners to use the six initials of the firm name (www.abcdef.com—instead of allenbox.com)—when the legal name is Allen, Box, Cutter, Davidson, Edmonton & Freehouse LLP. Try to rise above the politics and egos and choose a sensible, short name that is intuitive to find.

If you are currently using initials for your domain name, also register a more complete firm name, plus all its derivations. Do not make people have to remember the initials. *Note*: There are reasons NOT to change your URL, however—even though you want your firm name to point or redirect to "hjts.com." Changing your domain without keeping the old name and redirecting it to your website is damaging to your SEO.

Also register .net, .info, .pro, .biz, .us, .law, and .org versions—the price of name and reputation protection is worth the few hundred dollars this will cost. Get clever with your domain name for certain of your website assets—such as microsites and blogs. The State Bar of Texas and other state bar association advertising rules say that you cannot use names like www.thebestlawyerintx.com or winyourlawsuitinflorida.com. However, most, if not all, state bar associations enable you to create vertical, single issue or topic sites and call them antitrustlitigation.com, visalaw.com (the site of co-author Greg Siskind) or deregulation.com. Remember: your domain names are not merely locating devices—they have the capacity to convey a very important positioning and branding message.

Trademark and register all derivations of your domain name and firm name, including misspellings. Using the Allen Box firm example above, also register www.allanbox.com—to accommodate the well-intentioned visitor who misspelled "Allen." Think of your domain names as firm assets and intellectual property that should be protected.

Ten Foundational Best Practices for Law Firm Websites

5

As mentioned in Chapter 3, the Ten Foundational Best Practices (FBPs) are designed to give law firms a roadmap or checklist of things to consider the next time they refresh their website. Each of the Ten FBPs lists several attributes that are important to that FBP—they will give you assurance that your firm is offering the most visitor friendly experience possible. As noted, the FBPs and attributes are chosen based on broad website best practices, what we learn by tracking visitor behavior via Google Analytics, and what buyers of legal services tell us in interviews and focus group studies.

Content Pilot,[1] the sponsor and publisher of the associated research studies, chose the American Lawyer (AmLaw) 100 firms as the body of firms to evaluate in every study through 2013, although in 2016, Content Pilot researchers analyzed the Global 50 law firms. Most of the AmLaw 100 and AmLaw Global 50 firms are the largest firms in U.S. markets, are among the most recognizable brand names, and arguably have the budgets to purchase and design the finest websites around.

The 2016 research was completed in August 2016, and the comprehensive white paper, which includes trends and insights, do's and don'ts, and the results for each FBP, is available at no charge at www.contentpilot.com. The websites evaluated were those that were live on July 1, 2016. Sites that launched after this date were not included in the study.

The overarching question when conducting a research study year after year is, have things improved? In the case of these large, prominent firms, the conclusion

---

1. As noted earlier in this book, Deborah McMurray is the founder and chief executive officer of Content Pilot.

is mixed. Remember, these are *foundational* best practices—not the latest or coolest whiz-bang things. For many law firms, all of the FBPs and many of the attributes are "must-have," not "nice to have." When you are starting your new website planning, start with these foundational things.

SCORING OF THE 2016 GLOBAL 50 WEBSITES: TEN FOUNDATIONAL BEST PRACTICES STUDY

Nine researchers were assigned certain sections of the study to review based on their particular areas of website expertise. Each FBP and every attribute under it was individually evaluated for every Global 50 firm—70 attributes reviewed for each law firm website—and scored on a scale of 1 to 100. The attributes were averaged to create a total score for that FBP. Then the FBPs were averaged to reach the total score for each firm's website. Finally, all the law firm scores for every attribute and each FBP were averaged so we could report on how the Global 50 firms fared. In total, 3,500 attributes were analyzed for this body of firms.

For each attribute below, we list the average score of all the Global 50 firms on the 100-point scale. Also, at the end of each discussion, we include a chart that shows the breakdown of how all the firms scored, and the average for that FBP. Here is the scoring breakdown for each attribute:

- 85–100 = Excellent
- 71–84 = Good
- 51–70 = Fair
- 26–50 = Poor
- 25 and below = Unacceptable

FOUNDATIONAL BEST PRACTICE #1: COMMUNICATING YOUR MESSAGE

The first FBP in every research study since 2005 is Communicating Your Message, and the attributes evaluated were the following:

1. *Clear and differentiating positioning strategy* (meaning, do they put a unique and defining positioning stake in the ground—does the firm answer the question "Why should I care about you?" Is strategy evident? (See the earlier discussions about positioning in Chapter 2.) The 2016 Global 50 firms scored an average of **46**.
2. *Practice and industry focus are apparent* (it is a best practice to separate practices and industries—and it is advantageous to the firm to do so. According to the analytics we track, more visitors view industry pages

than they do practice pages (they self-identify as members of industries first)—it used to be three times higher, but this number has fallen. Law firms are not working hard enough to produce relevant, must-read industry content that the visitors cannot find elsewhere.). The 2016 Global 50 firms scored an average of **94**.

3. *Geographic reach is apparent (one office or 40).* The 2016 Global 50 firms scored an average of **93**.
4. *Contact information is clear and easy to find* (law firms do a much better job here than corporations or the Big 4/Next 4 accounting firms). The 2016 Global 50 firms scored an average of **59**.
5. *Site features or links to foreign language translations.* (All the firms boast that they are global—but how committed are they to their non-U.S. offices?) The 2016 Global 50 firms scored an average of **40**.

These attributes are entirely scalable to firms from large to small. If your practice is not global, then attribute number five above does not apply to you. If your clients are consumers, industry descriptions may not make sense—or they might—consider, for example, injuries in the energy, healthcare, or pharmaceutical industries.

Communicating Your Message as a best practice has essentially stayed the same since the first Ten FBPs study was introduced in 2005. The most troubling finding in the 2016 study was the dearth of firm strategy on the websites of these prominent law firms. The average score of all 2016 Global 50 firms on "clear and differentiating positioning strategy" was 46—or "Poor." Not having a unique and defining positioning strategy is a missed opportunity for firms to succinctly and compellingly tell their story, and to inspire their visitors to *feel* something about them.

It is as though with the rise of and easy access to new features and functionality, the largest firms are focusing on those (although the study results do not uniformly support this conclusion). It is challenging for firms to put that strategic positioning stake in the ground—it takes courage and confidence. And it makes some law firm partners uneasy—they would rather be something to everyone, which, given the size and reach of these firms, is not hard to do. (But what kind of strategy is "I want to be something to everyone?!")

Judging by this research and analyzing the large firm websites that have launched since the research was completed, too many firms have lost pluck when it comes to showing differentiating strategy on their websites—it means the large firms are increasingly looking alike. The AmLaw 100 firms performed much better on "strategy" in the 2007 study than the Global 50 did almost ten years later.

Yes, it is much harder to *not* be something to everyone—to define how you do business, your target markets, your growth plans, sweet spots, and the clients you are best suited to serve. Given that there are so few opportunities today to tell your unique story, it is recommended that firms not miss the chance to do a better job making a memorable first impression.

In the 2016 study, there were only seven firms that scored "Excellent" on this attribute. And 21 firms had no positioning strategy at all.

Thirty-one 2016 Global 50 firms had rotating carousels on their home pages, obviously a very popular and successful feature—and increasingly so. The carousel enables firms to showcase practices, industries, and other commitments and awards of the firm. Because of its high adoption rate in the legal industry, it is important that firms focus on making it unique to their firm—a differentiating strategy is the best place to start.

Note: The information featured in these carousels is often too firm-focused. Remember the question posed earlier, do your clients care about your awards and rankings? Carefully select the information to feature, such as client stories and important legal updates about which readers care. An excellent example of a largely client-centered carousel is the Winstead website (www.winstead.com).

Winstead's client-centered carousel

Another strong client-focused carousel (but a carousel that is controlled via right and left arrows by each visitor) is Merchant & Gould (www.merchantgould .com). This national intellectual property firm features client stories and the clients' products they protect.

Merchant & Gould's client-centered carousel

A good non-carousel example is Schiff Hardin (www.schiffhardin.com). All these sites perform equally well on smartphones as they do on a desktop, and the latter two sites, Merchant & Gould and Schiff Hardin, are responsive web design (RWD). More about RWD a bit later.

Schiff Hardin's non-carousel home page

All 2016 Global 50 firms boast that they are "global," but the average score of the Global 50 for having non-English translations was 40 on the 100-point scale.

The distribution of scores for Communicating Your Message

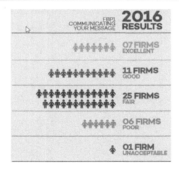

The total 2016 score for Communicating Your Message was 66.2—barely "Fair." This is down more than ten points from the 2010 study and also down from the 2013 study of AmLaw 100 firms.

Norm Rubenstein, a partner with the Zeughauser Group, and widely regarded as one of the legal industry's most experienced and innovative growth and positioning strategists, stated the following:

> Historically, law firm websites were difficult to parse, perhaps deliberately. Instead of articulating a positioning strategy that focused on one or more practices, sectors or geographies, most firms opted for an "all things to all people" approach.
>
> Today, however, in response to client demand, smart law firms are abandoning the "no child left behind" approach and finally are identifying the areas in which they legitimately can claim specialized expertise. That greater focus on the clear communication of memorable positioning strategy has given birth to a dramatic

shift in the ways that firms approach website content—including thought leadership. Now they spotlight the articles, blog posts and other indicia of their experience and expertise that highlight the areas in which they seek to be known as market leaders. And clients are benefitting from this shift by the ability to find, using Google searches and other research tools, the law firms best-suited when clients are creating their short lists in a given market (defined as practice, industry or geography) for a specific engagement or portfolio of matters.

FOUNDATIONAL BEST PRACTICE #2: DESIGN

This is the most subjective component of a website—do you say tomato or to-mah-to? What one lawyer loves, another hates; what one lawyer views as cutting edge, another lawyer views as garish and too fringe-y. So, how does your vendor hit the nail on the head for every law firm client? By focusing on strategy first. *Your* strategy.

The Graphic Design attributes from the Ten FBPs include:

1. *Bold, distinctively branded layout and style.* Most good designers design to this, but younger, self-trained designers miss out on this natural sense of "order." The average of all 2016 Global 50 firm scores was **61**.
2. *Strong, unique imagery reinforces and advances firm brand and story.* Ensure that your imagery does indeed enhance your story. Invest the time and money in images that will draw in your visitors and make them want more. The average of all 2016 Global 50 firm scores was **53**.
3. *Site is responsive with deliberately designed views for phones, tablet, and desktop.* RWD is now considered a foundational best practice, because it is the easiest way for firms with strapped resources (time and money) to satisfy visitors viewing on multiple devices. It is easy to recognize "old" websites, because they are optimized at a screen resolution of 1,024 x 768. Today, with RWD, the design stretches and shrinks to the screen size, so on your desktop the site appears very large, and on a smartphone the design shifts so that it will render well on the much smaller screen. The 2016 Global 50 average was **41**.
4. *Design is uncluttered and presents an intuitive information hierarchy.* Information hierarchy means having a clear understanding of what is most important on the page—what is next most important, and so on. It is up to your designer to ensure your most important messages are noticed first. The average of all 2016 Global 50 scores was **64**.

Twenty of the Global 50 websites were unresponsive, but the firms that had recent redesigns were all responsive. In the next Ten FBPs study, we are certain most will be responsive.

Many of the sites were old-fashioned in their page layout: they were divided into thirds—top third is the firm logo and banner/global navigation, then there is a rotating carousel of undifferentiating photos, then there are three vertical columns of "it's all about me" firm news, events, and awards. Do not settle on a rotating carousel just because it is hard to make a decision about what to feature. Make every feature compelling—and the carousel should not be complicated with too many buttons or views. Studies show that visitors view one or two items, seldom three, and never four.

The distribution of scores for Design

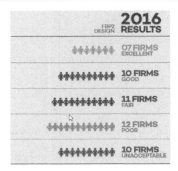

For the Design FBP, the 2016 Global 50 firms as a group scored 54.8 out of 100, for a grade of "Fair"—a pretty poor showing. The biggest design trend in the past three years is the wide adoption—or desired adoption—of RWD. Every firm writing a request for proposal for a new website wants a "responsive" website. So, what is it?

Responsive Web Design (RWD)

The undisputed leaders in online usability, the Nielsen/Norman Group (www .nngroup.com), define RWD below. We are including this rather technical definition because we think the gravity of this change in Internet marketing merits a more than superficial understanding of it. Note that not just websites are "responsive," but blogs, microsites, and social media sites can be, too.

Responsive web design (RWD) is a web development approach that creates dynamic changes to the appearance of a website, depending on the screen size and orientation of the device being used to view it. RWD is one approach to the problem of designing for the multitude of devices available to customers, ranging from tiny phones to huge desktop monitors.

RWD uses so-called breakpoints to determine how the layout of a site will appear: one design is used above a breakpoint and another design is applied below that breakpoint. The breakpoints are commonly based on the width of the browser.

The same [hypertext markup language (HTML)] is served to all devices, using CSS (cascading style sheets, which determines the design and layout of the web-page) to change the appearance of the page. Rather than creating a separate site and corresponding codebase for wide-screen monitors, desktops, laptops, tablets and phones of all sizes, a single codebase can support users with differently sized viewports. [Author note: the viewport is the part of the web page that is visible to you. And think of RWD as being the "what" and CSS is the "how."]

In responsive design, page elements reshuffle as the viewport grows or shrinks. A three-column desktop design may reshuffle to two columns for a tablet and a single column for a smartphone. Responsive design relies on proportion-based grids to rearrange content and design elements. [See the screenshots below.]

While responsive design emerged as a way to provide equal access to infor-mation regardless of device, it is also possible to hide certain items—such as background images . . .—on smaller screens. Decisions about hiding content and functionality or altering appearance for different device types should be based on knowledge about your users and their needs.

The Boston Globe was one of the first RWD sites, where the number of columns of story content would change from three to two to one, depending on the device used for viewing. Did it make sense for law firms to jump on the RWD bandwagon? Yes and, perhaps, no—regardless, they and the design/development companies have largely embraced the bandwagon.

RWD is not a panacea and you should be aware of its drawbacks:

- Depending on the number of breakpoints, your designer must create new wireframes and designs for each one. This can significantly raise the project management and design cost and time requirement of your website.
- Depending on the number of breakpoints, likewise, the development time is longer.
- You will need a longer testing period because the site must be tested on all devices—from your large, 24-inch screen desktop, down to the tiniest 4-inch smartphone—and the laptops, phones, and tablets in between. How is the performance on all devices? What if you are in a spotty area where there is little or no cell service and no WiFi, and you want to download your website onto your phone? Your content and design will perform less well under these conditions.
- Certain of your design choices and content will not make sense for your mobile visitors who want speed and only certain types of content. This means studying your analytics, understanding your audiences—what do they access, on what device, and from where—and feeding only the content they want. Many lawyers do not know their clients and prospects well enough to feel comfortable making such decisions. They really need to prioritize the content they are delivering.

Lindquist & Venuum, headquartered in Minneapolis (www.lindquist.com), is a good example of the use of RWD—as shown below on a desktop and iPhone 6s+. How is the desktop site different from the mobile site? Things to note:

- The desktop has traditional global navigation at the top of the page. The mobile site has a "hamburger" menu icon, which is what the collapsed menu as shown by the three bars is called. When you click on the hamburger menu, the global navigation menu appears, as shown below.
- The desktop has "Featured Practice" and "Highlights" sections. But on the mobile site, it just includes the Featured Practice.

Lindquist & Venuum's desktop home page

Lindquist & Venuum's mobile site

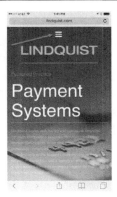

The arrow is pointing to the hamburger menu, and the image on the next page shows the hamburger menu expanded.

Lindquist & Venuum's expanded hamburger menu on its mobile site

Below is a second example of RWD (Keogh Cox & Wilson, Ltd. in Baton Rouge)—note the elements that are different from the desktop to the phone.

Keogh Cox & Wilson, Ltd.'s desktop home page

Keogh Cox & Wilson, Ltd.'s mobile site viewed on an iPhone 6s+

Once again, the global navigation is substituted with the hamburger menu on the mobile site. The home page carousel, which consists of three panels on the desktop site, is reduced to one panel on the mobile site; there is one news feature on the mobile site, where there are three on the desktop site.

For an example of a non-responsive website, see Chambliss, Bahner & Stophel, P.C.—Chattanooga (www.chamblisslaw.com). They launched a separate mobile design (from the desktop design) to offer tailored mobile content.

Chambliss, Bahner & Stophel, P.C.'s desktop home page

You can see that the number of global navigation categories is reduced from ten to four on the mobile site, but a visitor can access the full ten by pressing the menu button. Based on their Google Analytics and where visitors are spending the most time, Chambliss chose the most important four categories to feature. Plus, they did not sacrifice any of the positioning and branding by going small—"Jac," the black lab, still plays an important role on the small screen.

Chambliss, Bahner & Stophel, P.C.'s mobile site viewed on an iPhone 6s+

A Design Trend: Minimalism

From 2007–2010, the law firm design trend was to flow as much news and other fresh content to the home page as possible. There were advantages to doing this—namely, search engines favored these home pages over the static pages that never changed.

Starting in 2011, the rotating carousel took off, with more than 40 AmLaw 100 firms featuring them in the "2013 AmLaw 100 Websites: Ten Foundational Best Practices Study" and 31 in the 2016 Global 50 study. Law firms understandably appreciated the content flexibility and political correctness of the carousels. Several practices, lawyers, and news items could be featured at once. The downside is that there are not many design options to a carousel—so too many of these home pages from firm to firm looked exactly alike. And, in visitor studies, they admitted to not being patient enough to wait until all the carousel images/features cycled through.

There is now a move away from the rotating carousel, and designers, developers, and their law firm clients are seeking other ways to accomplish some of the same flexibility.

The Nielsen Norman Group conducted a 2015 study of 112 websites that were described by various web experts as "minimalist." Certain characteristics emerged, such as "flat design, limited color schemes, few UI [user interface] elements, use of negative space, and dramatic typography."

Flat design basically means they are not employing design techniques that produce shadows, gradients, or otherwise things that look three-dimensional. Not having this third dimension can sometimes be confusing to visitors because they are not sure whether, for example, a button that says "Go" or "Search" is clickable. When working with designers, ensure that they are not sacrificing good usability when making their design choices.

The 2016 Morgan Lewis (www.morganlewis.com) website can be described as both minimalist and employing flat design (although these terms are not interchangeable—you can have one without the other). In focus groups of corporate counsel, this website tests very positively because it is clean and easy to use. And, the Morgan Lewis website was the only one to score "Excellent" in the 2016 Global 50 study, with a score of 85.4.

The 2016 Morgan Lewis website, which employs flat design

FOUNDATIONAL BEST PRACTICE #3: NAVIGATION

Traditionally, global navigation (in the case of the Morgan Lewis example above, "Our Practices, Our People, Our Thinking, Our Firm, Careers") appears on every page of a website and it serves two functions:

1. It conveniently enables visitors to switch among top-level sections, regardless of where they currently are on the site. Global navigation is a grounding feature.
2. According to analytics and because of (primarily) search engines, visitors are increasingly entering your site on a page other than the home page. Global navigation can quickly help them preview what else they may view on your website.

There are three types of website visitors—searchers, navigators, and browsers. Searchers are visitors who, once arriving at your site, look for the search box. They generally know what they are seeking. Navigators are those who use your global and secondary navigation to choose the pages they want to view, and browsers are visitors who are shopping for where they want to go—searching some, navigating some, but typically touching several pages before they end up on the ones they want. According to what buyers of legal services say in client interviews, "Type A" people start with search—and if they cannot find what they want with your search, they try your navigation. Business people typically do not browse on their computers during the day, but they do browse on their tablets, and increasingly their larger smartphones, at night.

The scores for the Navigation FBP have significantly improved since the first AmLaw 100 research was conducted in 2005, but it actually went down in 2013. In 2010, AmLaw 100 firms scored 87—or "Excellent." With the updates made to this FBP in 2013, they only scored 71—barely "Good." And in the 2016 Global 50 study, it went down even further—the firms scored 50.

These firms are not keeping up with the standards set by the broad web industry or the expectations of website visitors. The highest score for this FBP was 91.3—and the lowest score was 37.5.

Visitors expect your site navigation to be, first and foremost, helpful. From then, it should be intuitive (meaning they can discern what they will find behind your navigation labels) and consistent from section to section.

The attributes for Navigation include:

1. *Global and local navigation styles are consistent.* A visitor does not have to relearn new styles throughout the site. It is maddening to visitors to have to guess where they should go once they land on a new page. Help them with their journey, by making it easy to navigate from one section to another. You can see in the examples below that the home page navigation (everything that appears above the red positioning strategy box that says "Projects that keep life moving") is easily carried over to the interior pages. The average of all 2016 Global 50 firm scores was **84**.

Kaplan Kirsch & Rockwell LLP's home page

An interior page from Kaplan Kirsch & Rockwell LLP's website

2. *It is easy and intuitive to navigate across multiple devices.* The mobile navigation tail is aging the desktop dog—hamburger menus are becoming more and more popular on desktop sites (another trend toward minimalism). Ensure that you do not lose intuitive navigation as your site scales down to tablets and phones. The average of all 2016 Global 50 firm scores was **64**.

3. *Site does not use multiple expand/contract features that hide valuable content.* Again, with an eye toward minimalism, designers want to hide content. It keeps the page design cleaner. The downside is that visitors cannot see that content and it can also be bad from a search engine optimization (SEO) standpoint. Some of the expand/contract features are good, but they must be balanced with broader usability goals. The average of all 2016 Global 50 firm scores was **79**.

4. *Site has a global footer with relevant clickable links.* It is surprising how few firms include global footers on their sites (other than the usual full firm name and copyright, plus the disclaimer and privacy notice). This is real estate that appears on every page—so it is a perfect spot for certain firm messages and news. It is also an intuitive spot for the complete site map to live. The average of all 2016 Global 50 firm scores was **35**.

The distribution of scores for Navigation

More about Navigation

Screen real estate typically prohibits more than six to eight global navigation sections. Consequently, some firms are designing two levels of navigation—*primary*, which typically includes people, industries, practices, news/events/publications, and then the rest is up for grabs. Certain firms include experience, multimedia, client tools, diversity, offices, blogs, and careers, plus others in the second level.

Secondary global navigation may appear in a smaller font and elsewhere on the site, such as in the upper right hand corner. Perkins Coie shows two levels of navigation in the upper right corner—primary navigation, which is larger (industries, etc.), and secondary, which is smaller (offices, etc.) and above.

Primary and secondary navigation at www.PerkinsCoie.com

Hamburger Menus

A trend for smartphone navigation is the use of "hamburger" menus. These typically appear as three, evenly-spaced horizontal lines at the top of the screen. (In the next image, we have circled the hamburger menu.) Touching it engages the menu and the global navigation areas appear. It is a clean way of handling what otherwise can be bulky global navigation labels on a small screen.

Below is an example of an RWD website, MB Law (Minor & Brown PC—www.minorbrown.com, headquartered in Denver), that uses a hamburger menu and also lists the global navigation titles on the home page.

MB Law's RWD website with hamburger menu

As with anything, there is a downside. According to the Nielsen Norman Group:

> Our user research with mobile devices has also identified many usability issues with specific hamburger designs even when used on phones, including inconsistencies, risk of activating the wrong part of the screen, and problematic representation of multilevel information architectures. Some of these issues can be overcome by closer attention to user-experience guidelines.

Nielsen Norman Group does not condone hamburger menus on desktop sites, believing "out of sight, out of mind"—if your navigation is concealed, your visitors will not click on the three bars and try to find out what is inside. The counter-argument is that visitors have been trained to know the hamburger menu includes global navigation—so they know what to do and where to find it on the desktop site. This does add extra clicks to their navigation experience, however. What is better? We are designing both ways—if the firm is what we might call "fashion-forward," we may suggest the minimalist hamburger menu. We like both.

FOUNDATIONAL BEST PRACTICE #4: PROFESSIONAL BIOGRAPHIES

These are the most important pages on a law firm website. Analytics prove that typically 40–70 percent of a website's total visitors view the lawyer biographies, compared to 6 percent, on average, for practice and service pages. It is surprising, however, how few lawyers take updates of their personal bio page seriously.

In the "2016 AmLaw Global 50 Websites: Ten Foundational Best Practices Study," the fourth FBP is Professional Biographies, and the ten attributes include:

1. *First 140 characters of the bio are current, compelling, and relevant for SEO benefit.* Count all letters, punctuation, and spaces and ensure that your most important keywords about your practice are appearing first. Avoid starting your bio like this: *John Smith is a partner and chair of the labor and employment practice at ABCXYZ law firm.* This is likely what will appear in the Google and other search engine results when searching by your name. This chair designation is important to you, but not as important to people evaluating you—do not waste this valuable Google real estate on your titles. Rather, tell what you do. Chris Jones's bio below is a good example—and you can see that Google pulls these first 150 or so characters when searching for his name. The average Global 50 firm score was **74**.

   Note: Because SEO is so important, we have an entire chapter devoted to it—Chapter 14. In this instance above, and the example below, we focus on "what" you do versus "who" you are. The fact that you are chair of your practice does not distinguish you from all the other chairs of labor and employment practices. Plus, this title will be prominently displayed elsewhere in your bio.

Chris Jones's bio at Keogh Cox

Search engine results for Chris Jones

2. *First two to three sentences of the overview describe the person's practice, client types, and industries.* After the 140 characters, focus on enriching your bio with additional keywords, such as types of clients, industries, and subject matter strengths. If you are a noted expert in Securities and Exchange Commission enforcement matters, Family Medical Leave Act claims, or elder law in nursing homes, this is where it should live. Peter Vogel's overview paragraph, below, is a great example—we have highlighted his overview in a box. The Global 50 firms did quite well on this attribute, scoring an average of **87**, which is "Excellent."

3. *Bio does not use Mr. or Ms. Lastname—it uses the professional's first or nickname.* What is more unfriendly than forcing a visitor to call you Mr. Hanson or Ms. Davison? The average Global 50 firm score was **60**. (Firms are reluctant to give this up, and it really is a throwback to 20 years ago, but it has improved—in the 2013 study, it was 35.)

4. *Photos are current and consistent, and convey the personality of the professional and the firm.* This was mentioned earlier under Design. It is critically important that your photos look like your lawyers. The average Global 50 firm score was **77**.

Peter Vogel's overview paragraph on Gardere Wynne Sewell LLP's website

Peter Vogel is renowned as both a trial and transactional lawyer who deeply understands technology, science and intellectual property – and the opportunities and problems they pose for clients. Governments and administrative agencies, major corporations and emerging businesses rely on Peter to get right to the heart of an information technology or e-discovery dispute – he knows what to expect and how it will play out in the courtroom. This eliminates unproductive rabbit trails and reduces the cost of litigation for all parties. When negotiating agreements for IT implementation projects for ERP or development projects for healthcare and other companies, his knowledge of technology enables his clients and their vendors to reach consensus faster.

5. *Full contact information is easy to find.* Make it easy for people to contact you. But—avoid the large, blinking buttons that scream "CALL ME!" Personal injury law firms often think these are a good idea—but they are not. The average Global 50 firm score was **99**.

6. *The professional proves accessibility.* The bio includes links to the lawyer's social media profiles and pages, which creates relationship stickiness. Understand your state bar rules about social media, but having the links on your bio page so visitors can easily connect with you is smart. Also include a virtual business card (vcard) and your assistant's name/contact info. The average Global 50 firm score was **91**.

7. *Bios list and crosslink to practices/industries and articles/news/events.* These encourage visitors to easily dig deeper into your qualifications and they guide your visitors on the journey you want them to take. The average Global 50 firm score was **89**.

8. *Bios include detailed experience and matter lists that are well organized and specific.* As noted before, buyers of legal services want to know what you have done, for whom you have done, it and what you can do for them. You must answer these questions before you can get hired. Period. Use client names if you have permission to do so, and be as specific as your state bar rules allow. The average Global 50 firm score was **79**.

9. *Page design displays elegant content organization that enables visitors to scan and consume what they want.* These are tools that designers and developers use to expand and contract content. It is sometimes referred to as hidden content, which will appear as soon as the visitor clicks on an arrow or button. In Marci Eisenstein's bio below, you can see the titles and arrows (for experience, etc.) in both a closed state and open state—to streamline design, this information is concealed until a visitor clicks on it and reveals it. Remember to not overuse these expand/contract features—maintain the right balance between streamlining and good communication and usability. The average Global 50 firm score was **81**.

Marci Eisenstein's bio on Schiff Hardin's website

An expanded view of Marci Eisenstein's bio on Schiff Hardin's website

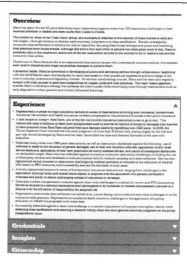

10. *Associates and professional staff have full biographies.* It was a many-year trend that New York and certain other American East Coast firms would list associates' names, but not include a bio for them. In interviews, clients complained about paying US$600 per hour for an associate that they could not even find on the firm website! This has changed, and most firms now include them, but the average Global 50 firm score was still only **71**.

You might think that the ten attributes above are a lot for Professional Biographies, but none of them are trendy or new. They are just smart building blocks to engage your visitors more—and to keep them on your most important bio pages longer.

The distribution of scores for Professional Biographies

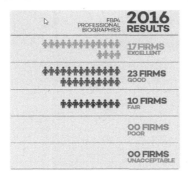

Create Three-Dimensional (3-D) Bios

Given that the majority of visitors are going to these bio pages, a law firm's goal should be to keep visitors on lawyer bios *longer*—and convert visitors to viewing more of them each visit. The bios are where the cash lives in your firm. Study Google Analytics or whatever tracking program you use and see how many different lawyer bios any one visitor opens, and check the average length of time a visitor spends on your bios. Then focus on improving this number and duration.

In today's landscape where competition among lawyers is steep, lawyers must provide more insight into why they should be hired. Why are they the expert? What makes them the perfect fit for a client's problem? You must prove you are the right fit, and there are three ways to do this:

1. Demonstrate expertise
2. Prove relevancy
3. Show humanity

All three "dimensions" must be present for professionals' biographies to work hard for them.

1. *Demonstrate expertise*
   a. Show *specific* experience: What have you done? For whom have you done it? What can you do for me?
   b. Include client case studies or stories that prove what you know and your approach to getting things done. This often gets into *how* you did what you did, not just *what*.
   c. Depending on the nature of your practice (for example, if you represent a lot of startups or technology companies), include client logos, with their permission, of course.

2. *Prove relevancy*
   a. Consistent with, and as noted above in the first attribute of FBP #4 (Professional Biographies), important keywords that are *relevant* to your practice appear in the top 140 characters (*characters*, not words) of the bio overview. When someone is Googling or otherwise searching for your name, it is important that the 140 or so characters that show up in the search engine description are the most relevant to your practice today—and the expertise that people are buying from you. Consider the disconnect for your future buyer if you are supposed to be the expert in global trademark protection and your Google search description does not even mention it.
   b. Current blog and Twitter posts feed into the bio. Social media that proves you are current and on top of the subject matter in your practice gives the people evaluating you comfort and confidence in your intellect and grasp of issues.
   c. Feature a book the lawyer has written—or something else notable, such as white papers, an important speech, or a short video about a trending topic.
   d. Design an infographic, which highlights trends in the lawyer's practice or industry. For example, number of patents in the energy industry over a ten-year period of time, or a U.S. map showing the number of states in which the lawyer has handled litigation.

3. *Show humanity*
   a. Shoot new lawyer photos—"magazine-style" (large format) photos that show personality and approachability. Some lawyers do not like getting their photos taken, so they use the same tired photo decade after decade. In today's world of selfies, where current photos are ubiquitous, it is critical that the firm website post current photos that *actually look like the lawyers* who work there.
   b. Include a short video that tells a memorable story about a case and how you handled it. Of course, do not name a client unless it is public record and you have your client's permission, but do discuss unique issues or circumstances. For example, did the case come in at 8:00 p.m. on a Sunday night and the court filing was due Monday morning at 10:00?

c. Include an "After Hours" tab or feature—content that describes the lawyer's passions outside the office. This can include community board service, volunteer work, travel, sports and events, books you are reading, the fact that you are training for a triathlon, or your pets.

d. Prove accessibility—include your assistant's name/info, your team's contact names/info (if you are not reachable, it ensures that your client has access to team members without you being a bottleneck) and instant messaging contact information. Law firm technology staff will sometimes prohibit instant messaging, but certain types of clients rely on it—and they want their lawyers to use it.

A good example of a 3-D lawyer biography is that of Dana Perry, the former managing shareholder of Chambliss Bahner & Stophel, where she lists her assistant, her team, and their contact information, and includes a "sidebar," which highlights her interests outside the office.

Dana Perry's bio page on Chambliss Bahner & Stophel's website (http://www.chamblisslaw.com/People/Dana-Perry)

FOUNDATIONAL BEST PRACTICE #5: CONTENT (EXCLUDING BIOGRAPHIES)

This FBP includes all other content on your website—careers, practice and industry pages, news, events, publications, about the firm, offices pages, and more. The attributes below should be applied to content on all these pages.

1. *Content is visitor-focused (not "all about me") and is available in multiple languages.* Paragraph after paragraph that show self-absorption are not interesting to readers. And, because many law firms present content this

way, it is another reason they all sound alike. Since the 2016 study focused on the AmLaw Global 50 firms, multiple languages is important. Obviously, if yours is a strictly U.S. law practice, you can ignore that piece of this attribute. The average Global 50 firm score was **80**.

2. *Page content has a clear information hierarchy and is well organized for the scanning reader.* Too many firms pay no attention to information hierarchy—they do not guide the visitor to what is most important on the page, what is next most important, etc. Visitors *want* you to guide them; it helps them save time.

3. *Practices and industries are broken out separately by services that clients buy; bonus for geographic regions.* (There is an example of regions shown on the Hogan Lovells site below.) There are advantages to designing two separate lists—practices, which is the work you do (mergers and acquisitions, lending, family law, intellectual property licensing, commercial litigation) and industries, which are the markets that define your client companies (transportation, aviation, health care, pharmaceuticals, software, real estate, banking). The advantage is that clients self-identify as a member of an industry (software) before they focus on the need they have (IP licensing). They want to ensure their lawyers understand their industry, markets, customers, unique challenges, and opportunities *first*, and then they want to talk about their licensing concerns.

   In addition, many lawyers default to the firm's organizational structure instead of thinking about what people are actually buying. For example, your real estate and banking services might be organized under a general corporate department. But a developer needing land use assistance or a lender needing a large loan documented are not going to look there. Break out these areas into their own descriptions and pages, "Land Use"

Hogan Lovells's practices menu

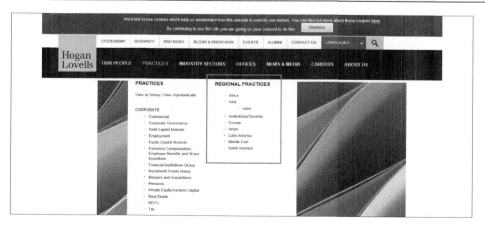

Waller's industries menu

and "Lending." And both of these examples could, or should, live under the global navigation area called "Industries" instead of "Practices." The average Global 50 firm score was **89**.

Waller does an excellent job of segregating their industries so that visitors in those fields can choose the subject matter expertise that fits their needs.

4. *Service descriptions include experience details and specifics.* Few firms told interesting stories about the clients they serve and the extraordinary work they do. However, when the content is more engaging, clients are likely to spend longer on your website, and the longer they stay, the more likely they are to trust your firm. The more trust, the greater likelihood that your firm will get hired or stay hired. Clients want to know what you have done, for whom you have done it, and what you can specifically do for them. It is no different than bios—add experience to your practice and industry pages. The average Global 50 firm score is **78**.

5. *Video and multimedia content is featured, well-produced, and short.* There are two goals here: (a) increase the amount of time visitors spend on your site, and (b) raise the odds of them digesting more content. These tools build engagement. If produced well, they showcase your lawyers' expertise, relevance, and humanity—a 3-D addition that will pay off. On websites that feature video and multimedia content, the analytics prove how much it is consumed and for how long. An excellent example is Eversheds Sutherland (merged February 1, 2017), which offers numerous videos and podcasts. The average of the Global 50 firms was **34**; in the 2013 AmLaw 100 study, the average was **37**.

A list of videos and podcasts available on Eversheds Sutherland's website (http://www.sutherland.com/NewsCommentary/Multimedia)

6. *Landing pages for news, articles, events, etc., are well organized and searchable by author, speaker, topic, date, etc.* The larger the law firm, the greater the visitor expectation is that you will provide multiple searches. To ensure greater consumption of your articles, etc., it is critical to include ways for visitors to sort and parse your offerings. The Global 50 average score was **89**.

7. *Site has a statement of core values related to the clients, the profession, and the markets served by the firm.* If your firm leaders live by your core values and you insist that all personnel do as well, then you should include them on your website. Your values about client service, responsiveness, excellence, and giving back help define and distinguish you. Excellent examples include Hogan Lovells and Reed Smith. The Global 50 average score was **92**.

8. *Site highlights the firm's commitment to diversity and inclusion.* While clients want the very best lawyers available to work on their matters, all things being equal, large companies want diversity in their outside providers. They track it internally and reward firms who care deeply about hiring and retaining a diverse workforce. The Global 50 did well on this, with an average score of **94**.

9. *Charitable and civic commitment is described and evident.* This is an area where you can brag about your passions and associations. Boast about your leadership positions on boards and prove your engagement in your communities. For local law firms, community leadership can be a compelling reason to hire one firm over another. Highlight your firm and lawyer leadership when describing your associations, and link to every organization you list. This is beneficial from an SEO standpoint. The Global 50 average score was **86**.

10. *Pro bono commitment is described in detail, highlighting stories and specific matters.* Describe your pro bono matters in detail with specific stories, outcomes, and links to lawyer and practice pages. This is another area where you can brag about your work and successes (following your state bar association rules, of course). The Global 50 average score was **88**.

11. *Every global section landing page is used as an opportunity for value-to-client messaging.* Too many sites were "all about me." There were a lot of undifferentiating, unproven, universally-used statements such as "We have the best people who do the best work who care the most about our clients." The Global 50 average score was **77**.

Practice and Industry Descriptions

The most disheartening thing about website practice and industry descriptions is proven by website analytics—visitors are not reading the practice pages. Depending on the law firm, views of these pages range from 6–8 percent—sometimes a bit lower or higher. The analytics historically proved that visitors viewed industry pages three times more than the practice pages, so breaking out industries from practices tended to drive higher consumption of those pages.

> *The most disheartening thing about website practice and industry descriptions is proven by website analytics— visitors are not reading these pages.*

However, in recent interviews with corporate counsel about how they use law firm websites, they are now admitting they are not favoring the industry pages— because law firms are not doing a good job delivering current, relevant information. (For many business-to-business law firms, it is still a best practice to separate practices and industries on your website, however. It enables firms to package their experience in different ways, and feature a more comprehensive understanding of the industries that are significant to your most important clients.)

This is a dilemma for law firms, especially the large, multi-service ones. How do they inform potential buyers and others about what they do? Law firm marketers and lawyers spend cumulatively tens of thousands of hours a year writing and updating these pages—for what? To be ignored?

The challenge (and opportunity!) for lawyers is to rethink these pages, understand what buyers are truly evaluating, and reshape and repackage your strengths so that they can be consumed as easily on a smartphone as on a desktop. Restructure the pages and provide content that does not merely inform—but *engages* your visitors.

The grades for the Global 50 firms should have been much higher on these practice and industry-related attributes. This is in part the reason why visitors are not consuming these pages—they are not getting what they want and need. In a day where people watch videos several times during their business days, if firms are not offering information via multimedia, they are off their radar screen.

When your firm is competing for work, against what firms are you most often competing? To see what prospects/visitors encounter, read your practice descriptions, then read the descriptions covering the same areas for your top three competitors. Do they sound alike? Do you handle mostly the same things? If you were a visitor, could you tell the difference firm to firm if you covered up the law firm names at the top of the pages?

Create a new "formula" for your descriptions, filled with information that is easily scanned and consumed. For example:

- Write a captivating overview that grabs readers' attention and fill it with keywords that are important to this practice. Tell what you do, then how you do it, as shown in the Keogh Cox business law and litigation description below.

An overview from Keogh Cox business law and litigation's page

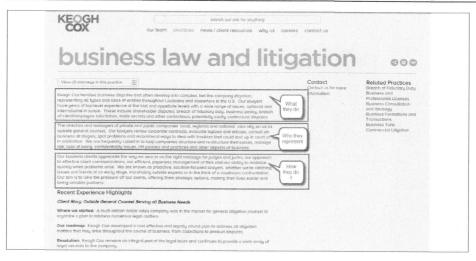

- Pay attention to the first 140 characters (as we have highlighted under Professional Biographies and the first bullet under "Prove Relevancy" in 3-D Bios above) for SEO purposes.
- Use bullets to highlight features, benefits, and results.
- Add short case studies that answer the questions who, what, where, when, and how. These will set your firm apart—they are, indeed, unique to you. Look again at the Keogh Cox business law and litigation example above—recent experience highlights include short client stories or case studies. These *prove* what you are saying in the earlier paragraphs.
- Bullet representative experience—a shorter, more concise version of who, what, where, etc.

An infographic from MWA Advisors' website

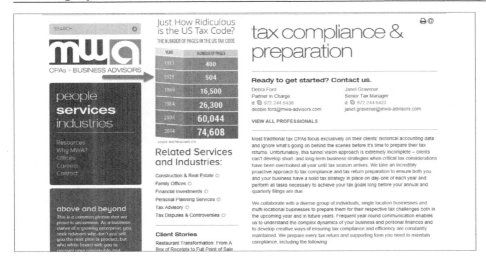

An infographic from MWA Advisors' website

- Add an infographic that tells a story about your work in this practice or industry. MWA Advisors is an accounting and advisory firm, which includes infographics on each service and industry page. Here are two good examples of how well this can work—one for a service area (tax compliance and preparation) and the other for an industry page (information technology and telecommunications).

- Include a primary and secondary lawyer contact name, with e-mail and phone number. These are the people who will be the most responsive and quickly refer an inquiry to the appropriate person. (Do not let your origination-based compensation system get in the way of referring visitors to the best and most responsive people.)

- Include links to related lawyers. Do not include everyone who has ever done one matter in this space—that is disingenuous to your visitor. Include your top, most experienced people. Associates can be included, too—and should be segregated in the search results (that is what appears when you click on the link to related lawyers), so partner contacts would be first and associate contacts second.
- Include links to other related practices and industries (e.g., M&A might have antitrust, corporate, and securities as related practices, and all industries for which you do M&A and you have a description, would be cross-linked).
- List and link related news, articles, events, and alerts.
- Add videos and podcasts that tell the story about the practice, cases, trending and horizon issues, a featured lawyer, and more.

News, Events, Publications, Press Releases, Articles, and More

Firms of all sizes invest heavily in publishing information about legal trends, new laws and regulations, cases in the news, industry, and market shifts. How many of these firms actually expect a return on this investment? Meaning, it is great that visitors are scanning the material (remember, they do not read—they scan), but is there conversion of this reader to a client?

Lawyers seldom ask how someone found them when they receive a new call. If your firm is investing in this thought leadership, track new phone calls that come in. They may be because someone received your name as a referral, went to your website to validate the referral, and found an article of interest. Then they picked up the phone or sent you an e-mail.

This is the goal. But you must track it to know if you are reaching this goal.

A Note about Press Releases

Too many law firm news releases are boasting about things that do not matter to buyers of legal services. What, for example, does winning multiple SuperLawyer or Best Lawyer awards do for a prospect? They make the *lawyers* feel good, but they do not move the needle for a client (as noted from years of client interviews). Include them, sure, but ensure that your firm publishes substantive material as well.

Headlines

The headline is the most important part of your news release or article. According to Elizabeth Lampert, president of Elizabeth Lampert PR, a national public relations firm serving law firms:

> The headline is the first thing and sometimes the only thing a reporter will read. Releases have been rejected on a weak headline alone, which is why, when writing the headline, you want to achieve the greatest impact using the fewest words.

Reporters are looking for salient information in the headline, so include who, what and why. Whatever the headline, it should accurately reflect the content that follows. Same rules apply for your first paragraph—cut through the clutter, tell them the news.

Below is a great example of a headline by Greenberg Glusker that grabbed the attention of a *Daily Journal* reporter—and the story ended up on the front page.

An article from Greenberg Glusker

Events

List upcoming and past events, including topic title, a short description of the event and content, date/time, location, hosts or the sponsoring organization(s), whether it is an in-person or online event, and how to RSVP. Publish the related slide deck and other handouts, and feature them on your website. Store it locally on your site or on a public presentation-sharing site, such as www.slideshare.net.

If your lawyers are polished, experienced speakers and presenters, videotape the presentation and post segments of it on YouTube or Vimeo. Create a special channel for your firm and start building a video library of current material. *Note*: if your lawyers are not very good speakers, do not post the videos—this can harm their reputation. (And, get them presentation skills training.) Rather, post a written synopsis and syndicate that in various social media.

Leverage the hard work your lawyers devote to preparing this material; tweet it, post it on LinkedIn as an update, and include a summary of the presentation and a link to the slides in an e-mail blast. Do not forget to syndicate everything you publish. This repetition is critical to establishing your firm and lawyers as the subject matter experts they are.

Even More Content

Law firms typically spend less time on the remaining content that commonly appears on a law firm website. These often include:

1. Careers—lateral hiring, summer associates/summer program, law clerks, and professional staff
2. About the Firm—a statement from the managing partner or chair, diversity, pro bono, community, office pages, and history

Analytics prove that careers pages are high traffic areas, with the .edu suffix ratcheting up your visitor numbers. If your firm does not have a law school recruiting program, it is still important to include pages that help interested laterals and staff find information about employment.

> *Analytics prove that careers pages are high traffic areas,*
> *with the .edu suffix ratcheting up the numbers.*

Law firms are understandably attached to their history, but in interviews with buyers of legal services, they admit they do not care much about it—they say they do not read it. They want to know your firm is stable and has a history of success representing clients similar to them, but beyond that, they say they do not care.

History is more for your *internal* audiences—lawyers and staff who want to feel good about the legacy of your law firm. It can also matter to your future employees. To make history more interesting to your clients, include a timeline of noteworthy cases, causes, and stories that relate to business—or the area of law(s) you serve.

Hogan Lovells's "Our Values" page (http://www.hoganlovells.com /ourvalues/)

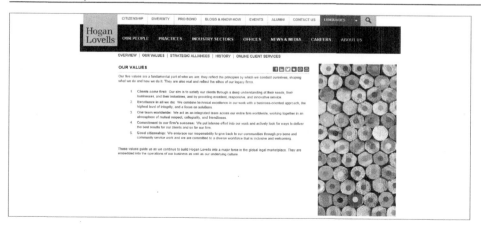

Reed Smith's "Culture and Core Values" page (http://www.reedsmith.com/aboutus/culture/)

The Global 50 firms do quite well on Content—much better than the AmLaw 100 did in the 2013 study. An average score of 81.2 on this attribute earns this body of firms a grade of "Good."

The distribution of scores for Content (Excluding Biographies)

FOUNDATIONAL BEST PRACTICE #6: INTERACTIVITY AND SOCIAL OUTREACH

This was added as an FBP in the 2010 study, when firms scored an average of 39, or "Poor." Social media was quite new, but was burgeoning like an amoeba. By the 2013 study—and certainly by 2016, it was expected that law firms would exploit the tools then readily available—having a successful social presence, being mobile, exploiting video and sharing environments, and the ability to subscribe to news feeds, alerts, and updates. The attributes are as follows:

1. *A client extranet is offered and accessible.* If your firm offers these sharing environments, place a visible link on your website and design a landing page that tells about the collaboration and sharing services you offer clients. Include the login box on that page. This is an opportunity to sell your technology and security capabilities, and to attract attention to how you work with clients. The average 2016 Global 50 score was **55**.

2. *Site includes a link to an alumni community (LinkedIn or separate website).* For several years, large firms were designing six-figure websites to attract their alumni—and then LinkedIn came along, which is a money-saver and the most efficient way to keep in touch with your former professionals. Your alumni are already keeping their profiles current on LinkedIn—do not make them come to your site and repeat those steps—save money and time for you, and time for them. Engage with them where they already are. Regardless, firms are not exploiting LinkedIn alumni channels enough. The average 2016 Global 50 score was **82**.

3. *Site includes newsletter subscribe feature, event registration, and other sign-up opportunities.* Including subscription forms for visitors to opt into receiving your newsletters adds some incremental cost to your website, but it is worth it to build and keep a following of important readers. Why publish if you are not effectively syndicating? The average 2016 Global 50 score was **73**.

On the Downey Brand website (www.downeybrand.com), the newsletter sign-up button appears on every page of the website, and the form is a good example.

Downey Brand's home page with a newsletter sign-up button

Downey Brand's newsletter sign-up page

4. *Site links to firm/lawyer blogs.* The competition for blog readership is up every year, so it is imperative that bloggers syndicate their blog posts wherever they can. The obvious place is the law firm website. Feed in the linked posts to the writers' biography pages, practice and industry pages, and news/articles/publications. Get as much attention for your blog posts as you possibly can. A good example showing blog posts fed into a bio and featured on its own tab is Gray Reed & McGraw, P.C. These are all posts by attorney Charles Sartain, who has a free-standing blog called "Energy and the Law." These posts appear as though they originate on the website, but they do not—they are RSS'd in from Sartain's blog. The 2016 Global 50 average score was **90**.

An RSS feed for Charles Sartain's blog on Gray Reed & McGraw, P.C.'s website (http://www.grayreed.com/Our-People/Charles-W-Sartain)

According to Kevin O'Keefe, founder of LexBlog, and Colin O'Keefe, LexBlog editorial manager, as of mid-year 2015 there were 78 firms blogging in the AmLaw 100 and they were producing 540 blogs.

5. *Site offers educational webinars, videos, and podcasts.* This is a missed opportunity for too many law firms. Turn your intelligence and skill into repeatable events, then post them on your website and drive traffic to them. Latham & Watkins offers more than 50 webcasts and podcasts covering, for example, Air & Climate Forecast, Securities and Exchange Commission: Focus on Controls at Public Companies, and Real Lessons from the Gulf Oil Spill Litigation. They offer them in non-English languages, too, which, given the global footprint of this firm, is very smart.

Webcasts and podcasts offered on Latham & Watkins's website (http://lw.com/webcasts)

Given the short attention span of virtually everyone today, develop a successful webinar and podcast formula and stick with it. Keep them short, to the point, and filled with practical information that will be immediately useful to your listener. For example, Eversheds Sutherland calls its videocasts "Bottom Line in 5 Minutes." This successfully sets the expectation that a visitor will not waste time. This formula also does not waste the lawyers' time in trying to reinvent the wheel. The average 2016 Global 50 score was **67**.

6. *The site links to social media sites and has an active presence there.* The first time social media link placement was measured was in the "2010 Ten Foundational Best Practices Study." Then, only one law firm included LinkedIn links on the lawyer biographies. Firms still are not doing a good job building relationships through social media—and they are, as mentioned before, missing a key bonding opportunity. The average 2016 Global 50 score was **66**.

7. *"Share" functionality is present throughout the site*. This is the best and easiest way to syndicate your content—and let others do it for you. (By clicking the share button, any readers who like your content can share it with any of their networks, such as Facebook, Twitter, etc.) It is a free and easy plug-in. Include it on every page. In the 2013 study, very few AmLaw 100 firms took advantage of this, but in 2016, firms were doing better. Thankfully, most new websites are including it today. The average 2016 Global 50 score was **71**.

Gray Plant Mooty's home page with a share button

The share menu on Gray Plant Mooty's website

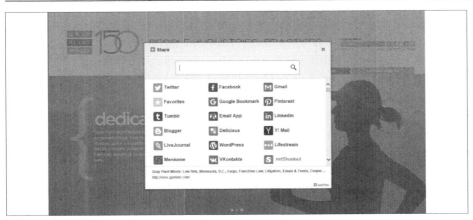

8. *Site offers a PDF "binder" or "build a brochure" functionality.* This functionality has been around for several years, but few firms invest in it. It enables visitors on the front end of your site to create their own packet of information about your firm—grabbing pages that matter to them, or their superiors. To help your site work harder as a business development tool, consider adding this functionality. The average Global 50 score was **7**.

For these eight attributes, the AmLaw 100 scores were low in 2013 (a score of 52) and they remain only "Fair" in 2016, with a score of 63.9. Law firms are not taking full advantage of the features and functionality that can drive more traffic, longer and repeat visits, and more loyal visitors.

The distribution of scores for Interactivity and Social Outreach

FOUNDATIONAL BEST PRACTICE #7: SITE SEARCH

Most law firms of all sizes give "search" short shrift. They place a search box in the upper right-hand corner and check it off their to-do list.

The must-have attributes are:

1. *Site offers an easy-to-find, full-site keyword search.* This box should prominently appear on each page and search all content on the site. Large firms do a better job than small firms here—it is surprising that even today, some websites are designed without a keyword search function. The average 2016 Global 50 score was **95**. All the sites had a keyword search, but some firm websites received points off because it was hard to find.

2. *Advanced search link or search options appear on all pages.* Remember, search is not about "searching," it is about *finding*. It is frustrating to type in a keyword and have a sea of irrelevant results returned. This is foundational functionality—you must give your visitors a chance to refine their search options so they receive only what matters to them. The average 2016 Global 50 score was **75**.

3. *Search results are clear and well organized.* Offer "faceted" search results—faceting is a way of organizing lists of information, so they are easier to access. Since analytics prove that visitors want to view lawyer bios first and more than other pages, organize your search results so that professionals or lawyers appears first. Typically practices, industries, or experience follow. A representative example of this is www.gardere.com. The Gardere search results are organized with professionals first, followed by experience, and highlight the keywords to make it easier on the visitor to determine relevancy. The average 2016 Global 50 score was **64**.

Gardere search results

4. *Site offers predictive search ("did you mean").* As noted above, the Gardere website highlights the search term "energy." Gardere also uses predictive search for its prominent home page search box. This helps visitors refine their search results on the fly. The average 2016 Global 50 score was **53**.

Predictive search results for "energy" on Gardere's website

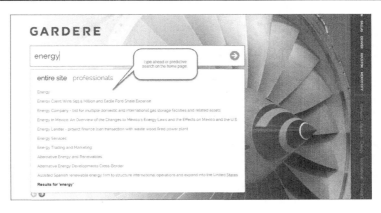

5. *Site offers a separate "experience" search.* Given that the burning questions in visitors' minds are "what have you done, for whom have you done it, and what can you do for me," it makes sense that mid-sized to larger firms would invest in separate "experience" searches (searching by keyword for the attorneys who have a certain type of experience), which require a feed of this data from a separate experience database. Make it easy to find and analyze your qualifications. The Eversheds Sutherland site below offers an experience search in the global mega-menu navigation, and a detailed search on every page of that section of the site. The average 2016 Global 50 score was a surprisingly low **14**, or "Unacceptable."

Eversheds Sutherland's experience search in the mega-menu navigation

Eversheds Sutherland's experience search in the mega-menu navigation

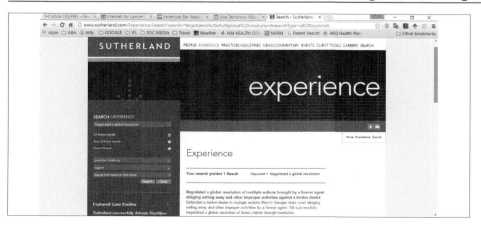

The average of the firms in the "How Do You Measure Up? 2016 AmLaw Global 50 Websites: Ten Foundational Best Practices" study was 60.2, or "Fair"—and 12 firms scored "Poor." Yes, high-performing search features add significant cost to your website—but given that virtually all of your visitors will be using them to find your content, it is worth the money. Only two firms scored "Excellent."

The distribution of scores for Site Search

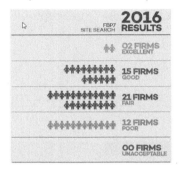

FOUNDATIONAL BEST PRACTICE #8: SITE OPTIMIZATION AND ONLINE AWARENESS (SEO)

Chapter 14 is focused entirely on SEO—and many of the terms used below will be defined in that chapter. Here, the focus is on basic things, *foundational* things firms must do to ensure their sites are getting the traffic they deserve. The Ten FBPs attributes for SEO, and the 2016 Global 50 scores, are as follows:

1. *High quality back-links and link relevancy are present throughout the site*: **100**.
2. *Site features strong, properly structured HTML content on the home page and interior pages*: **65**.
3. *HTML site maps are present and include all pages organized in a clear hierarchy*: **65**.
4. *Smart URLs with appropriate syntax are used in all sections*: **76**.
5. *Page titles, meta-descriptions, and natural keywords are used throughout the site*: **68**.
6. *Images have alt tags that provide alternative text when images cannot be displayed*: **56**.
7. *Tabbed bio and practice/industry pages all have the same page URL*: **72**.
8. *Correct schema markup is present throughout the site*: **12**.
9. *Site provides fast page load (less than 4 seconds)*: **81**.

Firms successfully avoided keyword stuffing and unnatural copy—one of the most prominent SEO (and human visitor) offenders. Firms that do this fall into the dreaded "black hat" SEO practices.

It was surprising to see so many of the world's largest firms without schema markup throughout their sites—this is an easy and useful addition, which should be implemented by all firms to boost their SEO. Schema markup is code that you put on your website to help search engines return more instructive results for users. It tells search engines what your content *means*, not just what it *says*.

Schema.org, the website for schema markup, was created by a wonderful inter-industry collaborative team from Google, Bing, and Yahoo. Learn much more about this at schema.org and on a blog that has successfully boiled it down for lay users called kissmetrics.com. Only six Global 50 firms used schema markup.

SEO success is an equalizer for firms of all sizes—and often small to medium-sized (and particularly business-to-consumer) firms out-rank the largest firms in keyword searches in the top search engines.

The distribution of scores for Site Optimization and Online Awareness

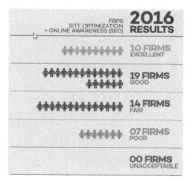

FOUNDATIONAL BEST PRACTICE #9: MOBILITY AND RESPONSIVENESS

Between the 2010 study and 2013, mobile usage became "foundational." Website analytics programs were tracking mobile usage, and the introduction of the iPad drove mobile traffic in ways we had not previously seen. When larger screen smartphones were introduced, more and more visitors were also accessing law firm websites on their phones.

Firms with recently updated or redeveloped sites kept mobility in mind far more than older, more outdated sites. Research shows that 2015 was the first year in which more Internet users searched on mobile versus desktop, proving the increasing significance of mobile design and usability. Users do not want to stretch their screens just to click links or read text, so all law firms redeveloping their sites must put a premium on superior mobile design.

For the "How Do You Measure Up? 2016 AmLaw Global 50 Websites: Ten Foundational Best Practices" study," the attributes are:

1. *Brand integrity is not lost on smaller devices.* A surprising number of Global 50 firms have not been strategic or deliberate in their design of the mobile version. Much of their branding on a mobile device is lost; logos and images do not show up in the right sizes or places, colors do not appear as they do on the desktop site, and text is often in long, scrolling blocks with no information hierarchy, making it difficult or impossible to find what you are looking for. Only 14 Global 50 firms scored 100 on maintaining brand integrity. The 2016 Global 50 firms scored an average of **70**.

2. *User experience is superior regardless of device.* Many sites do not resize on mobile, thus creating awkward and unfriendly spacing and making them difficult to navigate. Visitors must "pinch and zoom" to navigate and read the site's content, which is frustrating and time-consuming. The average score for the 2016 Global 50 firms was **59**.

3. *Mobile site features intuitive, well-spaced navigation tools.* The most important navigation advice is to ensure that "fat fingers" can touch one line or link and travel to where they want to go. It is maddening if your visitors cannot navigate accurately because of poor usability and design. The average score of the 2016 Global 50 firms was **60**.

4. *Content and images resize correctly and an information hierarchy is maintained.* Only 16 Global 50 firms scored 100 on content and images resizing correctly and maintaining a clear information hierarchy. The average score of the 2016 Global 50 firms was **59**.

5. *Mobile site is available in non-English languages.* This attribute may not apply to many of the readers of this book, but it does apply to the Global 50 law firms in this study. Only seven firms provided full translations on their mobile sites, with the ability to return to English, and 20 sites did not provide any language translations on their mobile sites, despite constantly promoting their "global" reach. The average score for the 2016 Global 50 firms was **36**.

The distribution of scores for Mobility and Responsiveness

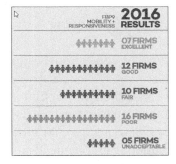

FOUNDATIONAL BEST PRACTICE #10: SITE "HYGIENE" AND USABILITY

This has been an FBP since the first study was done in 2005, although the attributes have shifted slightly. Site "hygiene" is about ensuring that your visitors have a trouble-free experience on your website. Any one of the attributes below is the technology equivalent of having spinach in your teeth or lint on your dark suit. The attributes include:

1. *Site perfectly functions on all modern browsers.* Remember that when you are testing your site to test it on small and large smartphones, as well as tablets, too. The average 2016 Global 50 score was **99**.

2. *Site offers dynamic print-to-PDF option on most pages.* Print-to-PDF functionality is common today—it enables the visitor to print a presentation-ready page directly from the website. It strips the HTML code on the top and bottom of the page, typically strips links, etc. Nineteen firms scored 0 on offering the print-to-PDF functionality—also surprising for 2016 law firm websites. We first scored this functionality in the 2005 analysis of the then-AmLaw 100 firms. We have not come very far it seems. Seventeen firms scored 100 on offering print-to-PDFs. The average 2016 Global 50 score was **47**.

3. *No error pages are found on spot check.* Errors are often created when you remove a page from your website and, in a Google or other search engine search, the link to that page still appears. A visitor clicks on that link, and is referred to a "Page not Found" message on your website. It takes a while for the search engines to update the pages they have indexed. Some of this is in your control and some of it is out of your control, but you should monitor it and fix it if it is within your control. The average 2016 Global 50 score was **100**.

4. *No broken links or images are evident with spot check.* If you are cross-linking inside your site or otherwise linking to other material in your site, ensure they are all working. Same with images—ensure that the little red X is not appearing instead of your photos or illustrations. The average 2016 Global 50 score was **97**.

5. *Pages print and e-mail easily.* This is such important and basic visitor-friendly functionality, it is surprising that the Global 50 firms did not score 100 on this attribute. Provide the page tools that let your visitors further engage with your website. In the study, e-mail functionality was often hidden under share options, if it was offered at all. Frequently, the only option was to share via social media, but not to e-mail to another person. The average Global 50 score was **60**, or "Fair"—a very poor showing for this important feature.

6. *Content has been checked for spelling.* Every firm, regardless of size, should score 100 on this attribute. It is often difficult to proof your own work (and website copy); consider hiring a proofreader who can scour every page of your content before you launch.

Post-launch, there are spell-check plug-in tools that you can install on your site. There are free online spell checkers, as well as various tools that you can purchase. Most are good or very good, but none are perfect—human oversight is still recommended. The average 2016 Global 50 score was **97**.

7. *All appropriate domains are active, including HTTPS.* We are seeing more and more law firms wanting to launch their new websites using HTTPS instead of HTTP. This extra layer of security gives law firm leaders and the information technology professionals more comfort. Users expect a secure online experience when they are providing data via a website, whether they are ordering tickets to a concert, buying shoes, or subscribing to your law firm's newsletter. We encourage you to adopt HTTPS in order to protect your users' connection to your website. The 2016 Global 50 firms scored **100**.

8. *Site meets W3C Level 1 accessibility standards.* This is the first study in which we have tested website compliance for those with disabilities. Testing the Web Content Accessibility Guidelines (WCAG 2.0) sponsored by the Bureau of Internet Accessibility (boia.com), we found that compliance varies immensely from site to site, but is generally strong among the Global 50.

BoIA states:

Trying to understand the WCAG 2.0 Guidelines can be confusing, not to mention trying to figure out how they relate to the [Americans with Disabilities Act], [Accessibility for Ontarians with Disabilities Act], Section 508 [of the Rehabilitation Act] and other compliance requirements. Putting the remediation into place to make your website accessible can get laborious as you try to weed through the requirements and implement the changes needed. On the BoIA website, you can enter your URL and your site will be graded using the WCAG 2.0 Success Criteria and graded using the four principles: Perceivable, Operable, Understandable and Robust.
The WCAG 2.0 Success Criteria includes:

- Perceivable information and user interface components must be presentable to users in ways they can perceive.
- Operable user interface components and navigation must be operable.
- Understandable information and the operation of the user interface must be understandable.
- Robust content must be robust enough that it can be interpreted reliably by a wide variety of user agents, including assistive technologies.

If you want a full content audit of your site, contact sales@boia.com.

Only 12 firms scored 100 on compliance with the W3C Level 1 guidelines. The 2016 Global 50 ranked "Excellent" on this FBP, with a score of **87**.

Do not let your website fall victim to users' negativity biases. Many scientific studies document negativity bias, which is defined as:

The tendency for humans to pay more attention, or give more weight to negative experiences over neutral or positive experiences. Even when negative experiences are inconsequential, humans tend to focus on the negative.

According to Nielsen Norman Group, the global gurus of website usability, this is what negativity bias means on the web and to your firm:

A single usability flaw on your site will weigh more than the many positive features that you've struggled to implement. To leave a lasting positive impression, user interfaces must not only be good, they must be great, and you must root out every single design flaw with a vengeance.

The distribution of scores for Site "Hygiene" and Usability

The total scores for Content Pilot's "How Do You Measure Up? 2016 AmLaw Global 50 Websites: Ten Foundational Best Practices" study are below.

Content Pilot's 2016 total scores

If you are interested in receiving a copy of the comprehensive white paper about the "2016 Global 50 Websites Study," please visit www.contentpilot.com /subscribe for a free download.

6

Website Technologies and Platforms

There are numerous platforms or content management systems (CMS) available for your website, ranging from proprietary (licensed products) to open source (licensed, but non-proprietary). We define each one in more detail below. Very simply, a CMS is, according to Wikipedia, "a computer application that allows publishing, editing, modifying, organizing, deleting, and maintaining content from a central interface. Such systems of content management provide procedures to manage workflow in a collaborative environment."

According to various sources, such as CMS Matrix and Capterra, there are between 1,000 and 1,200 different CMS platforms. Mid-sized to larger firms often hire vendors that have developed their own tools—some specifically for law firms—but many smaller firms also find these proprietary tools to be an advantage over more generic something-to-everybody ones.

OPEN SOURCE

With the proliferation of WordPress (www.wordpress.org) as a dominant website and blog platform (WordPress claims to power more than 23 percent of the web), and Drupal (www.drupal.org) as a website CMS, and the relative ease of developing on them by many, many developers throughout the United States, "open source" has become a popular choice for websites of all sizes. It refers to a broad and general software license that makes source code available to the general public with relaxed or non-existent copyright restrictions.

This is the spirit of the definition established by the Open Source Initiative (www.opensource.org) in 1998. It does not necessarily mean free—in fact, free software is a sub-set of open source. WordPress and Drupal, however, are free, but the templates and plug-ins are not.

According to the Drupal website:

> Drupal is open source software maintained and developed by a community of over 1,000,000 users and developers. It's distributed under the terms of the GNU General Public License (or "GPL"), which means anyone is free to download it and share it with others. This open development model means that people are constantly working to make sure Drupal is a cutting-edge platform that supports the latest technologies that the Web has to offer. The Drupal project's principles encourage modularity, standards, collaboration, ease-of-use, and more.

Developers can manipulate, create, design, alter, and adjust the open source software without infringing on the copyright. WordPress, Drupal, and other open source platforms, such as Squarespace (www.squarespace.com) and Joomla (www .joomla.com), which are also free, include content management systems, but the CMSs are not tailored to the unique needs of law firms or professional services firms. Experienced developers can customize the CMS to be a law firm fit, but the end result is a retrofit—sometimes the result works well and sometimes it does not.

According to various developer reviews, the top three free software offerings stack up as follows: WordPress is at the "user-friendly/looks pretty/basic tasks are easy" end of the scale. Drupal is at the "incredibly customizable/developers love it/ slight learning curve for mere mortals" other end. And Joomla falls somewhere in the middle. According to one online review by Bill Powell, a content management system expert, (http://cms.about.com/od/cms-basics/a/Pros-And-Cons-Of-Joomla -Wordpress-And-Drupal.htm) "If you know you'll want extra features on your website, Joomla isn't the best choice. The Joomla community offers tons of modules, but they are currently hard to find and harder to maintain. Both WordPress and Drupal have a much better handle on this system."

WordPress sites start with a "template" or "theme," and, from there, developers can plug in numerous widgets and tools that add features and functionality. The other platforms work pretty much the same way. This plug-and-play development approach for websites sounds fast, cheap, and easy, but it may not be any of the above. WordPress, for example, has more than 15,000 plug-ins. Most developers do not have the time, capacity, or interest to research more than a handful of them, so they often will re-use what they have used before. The themes can be very restrictive (meaning they are hard to change and manipulate) and, thus, the resulting website may have a cookie-cutter look to it. Literally tens of thousands of websites have started with the same theme. The structure will be the same or similar and the layout can look the same. Your law firm website may look similar to the site of your local wedding planner, master gardener, cookbook seller, and pet sitter.

Security is a hot issue for law firms and their clients. There is a school of thought that open source software has the potential of greater security risk and hacking by nefarious people because hundreds, perhaps thousands, of developers are developing plug-ins and modules for these platforms, hoping to cash in (literally) on the platforms' popularity. For most law firms and many of their developers, it is not feasible to know exactly what you are getting when you purchase a plug-in—is it infected or not? At the very least, developers hired by the law firms should be experienced with a stable list of clients who continue to use them—and they should know the correct use of core application programming interfaces (APIs) and the underlying server configurations. Not paying attention to them can put your site—and your firm—at risk.

PROPRIETARY PLATFORMS AND CONTENT MANAGEMENT SYSTEMS (CMS)

The legal industry has several companies, such as author Deborah McMurray's company, Content Pilot, as well as Rubenstein Technology Group, FirmSeek, and Saturno, plus others, that have developed content management systems specifically for the unique functions (such as bio management and multiple cross-linking) of law firm websites. There are other companies that use, as a starting point, a CMS platform called SiteCore- Experience Platform/ (www.sitecore.net), which is an enterprise platform used by major corporations and several American Lawyer (AmLaw) 100 law firms. Certain website development companies that serve the legal industry only develop on SiteCore.

Skilled SiteCore developers say there is no limit to what it can do in terms of managing huge sites, multiple sites, and sites in multiple languages. The community of users and support is growing and there are increasingly more tools being developed for it. It is expensive to license, and pricing follows a flexible licensing cost model based on the size of the law firm's CMS (determined by the number of SiteCore servers required) and the number of simultaneous law firm users logged in.

There are several established companies that work with law firms and provide successful proprietary platforms. In some cases, the CMS is designed specifically to accommodate the unique needs of a law firm and its website. When considering hiring a company that sells a proprietary platform, ask:

1. What platform is it built on?
2. How many years old is the current version of their platform? If the developer is not keeping the platform updated, even three or four years old can be "old" by today's standards.
3. What updates have they made to the platform recently, when, and what were they?

4. How many law firms are using this platform?

5. What are the licensing arrangements and post-launch support that you will receive? Every website needs care and feeding—there will be both issues that arise and updates that need to occur, and you will want to change design or the layout of certain sections of the site. Your post-launch support should be clearly defined or you may be surprised by the high cost of "maintenance" fees. Will they update your website platform post-launch? "Under the hood" system updates must always be handled by your developer. These are very different than the content updates that you will handle on your own.

7

Website Timelines, Budgets, and Contracts

All lawyers want the website to take less time to design, develop, and launch. As noted in Chapter 4, it can take as little as three months for a simple site and more than a year for one with complex features, functionality, and integrations. What often causes these projects to languish is content not being finished. Many firms take the opportunity to "clean out their content closets" during a website refresh—very smart decision. Start this culling process as soon as you can, as it always takes longer than you think.

Why spend the time and money migrating content that is not seeing the light of day? Take a critical look at every page of your content—for mega-firms, this is a tall order, but your visitors will thank you. It means they will not receive countless irrelevant content pieces when they do keyword searches on popular terms. You are saving your visitors valuable time. They will notice and like that.

Using the typical website phases or steps noted in Chapter 4, the suggested time each takes has been added below.

TYPICAL PHASES OF YOUR WEBSITE AND THE TIME EACH TAKES

In Chapter 4, we outlined the typical phases of your website. Here, we outline them in the context of how long each phase can take. Our goal here is to help you set and manage expectations in your law firm—these projects take time and patience.

1. *Statement of work and scope of work (SOW) discussion*—The statement of work is the statement about what the work is, but also, how it will be performed, how long it is anticipated to take, etc. The scope of work is simply what is included in the project. Typical SOWs include a line item, such as "Design"—and a description of how many unique pages are included, how many concepts will be presented, how many breakpoints if it is a responsive site, and how many design revisions are included on each page.

   It takes time for the vendor to prepare the contracts and to work with the reviewing lawyer or procurement contact to finalize them. This can take as little as two weeks and as long as eight or more weeks (large firms take more time than smaller firms—the contracts are essentially the same from large firms to small firms, it is just that the process of review has more steps in the large firms).

2. *Strategy*—As noted earlier in this book, strategy is a critical component of successful website engagements. This may be a separate phase and consulting engagement that precedes the website planning. If that, it could occur two or more months before the website planning begins. If done in conjunction with the website kick-off meeting, it might only add a week or two of extra time.

3. *Site architecture, wireframes, and technical requirements*—Depending on the complexity of your site, this phase can take from one month to three or more months. Remember, these are critical documents to the successful completion of your site (comparable to the architectural documents for your home). "Templated" sites may not require separate site architecture and wireframes because the site structure, features, and functionality have been predetermined. Custom sites will almost always require these documents, which help the design and development teams to understand how the site is supposed to perform.

4. *Graphic design*—The time required depends entirely on how many unique pages your site will have. Ten unique pages takes about half the time as 20 unique pages. Your design team will start by presenting initial designs (up to two to three design ideas or concepts), then prepare up to two rounds of revisions of the chosen design. The timing of these approvals—how fast or slow they happen—is often what causes this phase to extend project timelines. That, and whether firms seek consensus on the designs from many partners, as opposed to a selected website committee that is tasked with this responsibility. The other thing that causes delays in this phase is requiring more rounds of revisions—this adds both time and cost to your project. Additional rounds of revisions *will* cost more money, so do not ask for these lightly. Coordinate and aggregate the revisions, so you can stay within the approved SOW.

5. *Design consistency review*—This depends on the size and complexity of the website, too. This can take one week for a smaller site and two

months for a large, enterprise site. If you are launching additional website assets at the same time (microsites, mobile site, blogs), these all add time to this phase. Do not skimp on this phase—it is critical to your visitor experience.

6. *Programming*—Depending on the complexity of your site, this often takes two or more months. It can take up to four or five months, or even longer—again, depending.

7. *Content migration*—This is an arduous task, which includes migrating content from your current site, as well as adding new content by hand. For large sites and for multiple website assets, this may be done as a team effort—your firm employees or contractors, plus your vendor team. Plan ahead to ensure you allow enough time. Imagine migrating 10,000 or more pages—it takes a long time to get it right. Plan on two weeks for a small site and up to three months for a large (or multiple site) project.

8. *Testing*—Alpha testing, the period when your vendor team tests the site, can take from one week for a small site to six to eight weeks for a large site. Beta testing, or user acceptance testing (UAT), is when the law firm has its chance to scour the site, make last minute content changes, and so on. This is an iterative process, where the firm tests things, sends changes back to the vendor, which makes the changes, then sends it back to the firm where they continue to test. Plan on two weeks minimum for beta testing, and for larger and more complex sites (or multiple sites), plan on at least four to eight weeks of beta.

9. *Pre-launch and launch*—The pre-launch time is when the final changes are made by the vendor and the site is "locked down," or unavailable to the firm to make any more pre-launch adjustments. It is also when the firm's internal technology staff works with the vendor to make the Domain Name System (DNS) transfer. Plan on two days minimum for a small site and up to one week to ten days for a large/multiple site project before you can actually launch your site.

CONTRACTS THAT GOVERN YOUR WEBSITE PROJECT

The required contracts vary from vendor to vendor, but a firm should expect to review and sign the following:

1. *Master services agreement*—This is the document that governs the terms of the vendor/client relationship and includes the positions around confidentiality, termination, bankruptcy, how the work will be performed, amendments and change orders, payment and terms, delivery and acceptance, warranties, ownership of intellectual property, indemnification, and perhaps others.

2. *Statement of work and scope of work (SOW)*—The acronym SOW is often used interchangeably for both terms. The statement of work outlines every aspect of the website engagement and what you should expect to receive. This should be completely unambiguous and spell out exactly what you can expect for each phase of your project, including the hours and cost to which you have agreed. It will also outline payment terms, which typically begin at the signing of the contracts, and continue with the final payment 30 days after launch. The SOW document should include a change-order form that will be used if you find a need to add functionality or increase the scope of the project. Your final payment will include the final scheduled payment, as well as the cost of SOW enhancements.

3. *License agreement*—If you are working with vendors that develop websites using their proprietary software, they will require the firm to sign this agreement. This presents the terms of using the vendor software (this may range from one year to three years and be renewable), and typically includes sub-headers, such as the license grant, use restrictions, archival copies, license term and renewal, infringement, enhancements to the software that the vendor may provide, fees, warranties, confidentiality, and liability.

4. *Service level agreement (SLA)*—This is the document that governs the relationship after you launch your website. It provides a description of the services and the user environment, responsibilities, and support services available to clients related to the website implementations. The SLA should include a discussion of scope of the services, definitions/acronyms/abbreviations, service descriptions, dependencies and metrics, non-emergency enhancements, scheduled maintenance, normal business hours, after hours access, and escalation.

5. *Hosting agreement*—As soon as your website is transferred from a development environment to a "staging" or "production" environment, you will be responsible for paying hosting fees. Your vendor may host your site (often through a third party service) and provide management services along with it, which means this agreement would be provided by your website vendor. The hosting cost in this instance will be hosting plus the management services cost.

   This document typically covers the hosting term and payment for services, termination policy and liability, a description of the services provided, bandwidth and usage, backup and recovery, restoration of service, domain names, security, data retention upon termination, availability, intellectual property rights, other obligations and disclosure rights, interruption of service, warranties, and perhaps more.

BUDGET

As detailed in Chapter 4, there are numerous variables that will drive the cost of your project. Asking what a website should cost is similar to asking how much a house or car should cost. It depends entirely on what you are buying, from whom you are buying it, and in what region of the country or world your purchase is made.

Certain vendors charge solely based on time and materials. Others do that, plus they may have certain tasks for which they will charge a flat fee, regardless of the time they spend on it. Some vendors will under-bid simply to get hired, but may bait-and-switch you later on—up-charging you for things that should have been included at the get-go.

Request budgets from two or three short-list vendors with proven track records in the legal industry, and try to evaluate the budgets apples-to-apples as much as possible. Often you will receive a low, medium, and high range for the same work. This does not mean you should always hire the lowest priced provider—evaluate their references, website history, understanding of lawyers and law firms, chemistry you have with their key employees, service philosophy, and the value-added services they provide pre-and post-launch. You may ultimately feel most comfortable with the highest priced vendor.

Scope creep is common in website and other software development, mostly because the people scoping the engagement did not know enough about it. Avoid this by carefully negotiating the SOW before you sign any contracts, and lock in your price for the specified services you expect to receive. Ensure that any SOW enhancement is covered by a jointly executed change-order, so you eliminate scope creep surprises later on.

Website Hosting

8

Where you host your site is a critical decision. You are seeking maximum reliability and up-time of your most important and public business development asset. Your options are to host your website on an internal server that you own or to hire a third-party company (often your website design/development vendor).

Ask these questions when deciding whether to host internally:

- Do we have excess bandwidth coming into our offices?
- How stressed and stretched are our technical resources? Are they keeping up with their current information technology (IT) responsibilities?
- Do we have the IT staff who are knowledgeable enough to manage the hosting environment 24/7?
- Does our firm have the firewall security in place?
- What is the purpose of the website? Will we grant access to password-protected information and content on a select basis?
- What level of traffic do we expect?

ADVANTAGES OF EXTERNAL HOSTING

- This is the hosting company's core business, not yours, and many of the largest hosting companies have proven track records that you can review.
- If your internal server crashes, your number one sales, marketing, and recruiting tool does not crash with it.

- Unlimited bandwidth, regular and frequent back-ups, and power redundancy means your site should be available 24/7. Some companies automatically mirror sites on remote back-up servicers, in case of disaster.
- Some web development companies, as noted, provide hosting services—and with them, sophisticated tracking and analytics. These people can help you analyze and understand your site's traffic, so you can view your future enhancements and content improvements more strategically. These companies—because they have a long relationship with you—often provide better service than large "retail" hosting companies, such as GoDaddy. If your site goes down, you have a project manager you can call, someone with whom you have worked, who can tell you what is happening. In many instances, you will be notified by them, because they receive instant notification of outages from their service providers.

There are hundreds of hosting companies, and with the option of hosting in the cloud, more are popping up every day. Focus on their track records before you focus on the cost. Cheap often comes at a price you would rather not pay.

HOSTING IN THE CLOUD

Cloud hosting has become a serious alternative to conventional servers, because it is a cost effective storage solution that is flexible, reliable, and scalable. It can cost less than conventional servers, but this is not guaranteed. Corporate America has largely moved to cloud hosting, with many large companies investing heavily in on-premises cloud hosting environments.

Cloud hosting services can be utilized from an off-premises service or deployed on-premises. Excellent hosting options are increasingly available in the cloud, such as Amazon (yes, the same Amazon that ubiquitously sells you books, music, movies, and children's toys) Web Services, or AWS. AWS promises that it will "help you get your applications up and running faster while providing the same level of security that organizations like Pfizer, Intuit, and the US Navy rely on. AWS also provides resources around the world, so you can deploy your solutions where your customers are." For global law firms with global clients, 24/7 site availability is even more imperative.

As an example, AWS offers various tiers of service—basic, developer, business, and enterprise, which includes defined response times ranging from several hours to an immediate phone call. "Developer"-level support is available via e-mail Monday through Friday, 8 a.m. to 6 p.m. in the customer's time zone. "Business" and "Enterprise"-level customers have access to support at any time, 24/7, and 365 days per year via phone, chat, and e-mail. The cost associated with this availability is commensurate with the services and access provided.

Data security is increasingly important, as major news outlets report of data breaches of huge organizations (Target, Citicorp, JP Morgan Chase, Home Depot, UCLA Health System, and Harvard University, as examples) and the U.S. Government (Internal Revenue Service and Office of Personnel Management)—and even prestigious law firms. Large law firms are at risk, because of their having access to and storing their clients' confidential information. Large cloud hosting companies invest tens (perhaps hundreds) of millions of dollars in security every year, which benefits each of their customers regardless of size who pays for their services. They are also updating their software and frequently replacing hardware with the latest processors that not only improve performance and speed, but also include the latest secure platform technology.

In a March 2015 blog post by Cloud Academy (http://cloudacademy.com/blog /disadvantages-of-cloud-computing/), among the top disadvantages of cloud hosting or computing are:

1. Downtime—This may be one of the worst disadvantages of cloud computing. No cloud provider, even the very best, would claim immunity to service outages. Cloud computing systems are internet based, which means your access is fully dependent on your Internet connection. And, like any hardware, cloud platforms themselves can fail for any one of a thousand reasons.

2. Security and privacy—. . . your cloud service provider is expected to manage and safeguard the underlying hardware infrastructure of a deployment, however remote access is your responsibility and, in any case, no system is perfectly secure. You'll have to carefully weigh all the risk scenarios. After the recent leaks of celebrity pictures and countless millions of user login credentials, the privacy of your cloud-based data is another consideration. How much can you trust your provider? Can you face this, which is one of the riskiest disadvantages of cloud computing?

3. Vulnerability to attack—In cloud computing, every component is potentially accessible from the Internet. Of course, nothing connected to the Internet is perfectly secure and even the best teams suffer severe attacks and security breaches.

4. Limited control and flexibility—To varying degrees (depending on the particular service) cloud users have limited control over the function and execution of their hosting infrastructure. Cloud provider End User License Agreements (EULAs—often more simply referred to as software license agreements) and management policies might impose limits on what customers can do with their deployments. Customers are also limited to the control and management of their applications, data, and services, but not the backend infrastructure. Of course, none of this will normally be a problem, but it should be taken into account.

5. Cloud computing platform dependencies—Implicit dependency, also known as "vendor lock-in" is another of the disadvantages of cloud computing. Deep-rooted differences between vendor systems can sometimes make it impossible to migrate from one cloud platform to another. Not only can it be complex and expensive to reconfigure your applications to meet the requirements of a new host, but migration could also expose your data to additional security and privacy vulnerabilities.

6. Cloud computing costs—Cloud computing—especially on a small scale and for short term projects—can be pricey. Though it can allow you to reduce staff and hardware costs, the overall price tag could end up higher than you expected. Until you're sure of what will work best for you, it's a good idea to experiment with a variety of offerings.

Announcing, Promoting, and Growing Your Website

9

While a web marketing plan should include tactics to keep your website top-of-mind in your target audiences, the best way to keep visitors coming back is to keep your content fresh—*very* fresh. In addition to your fresh content, consider the following ideas to promote the launch of your website:

- Give away a signature toy with the firm's URL on it.
- Send an e-announcement that gives readers a tour of site highlights.
- To engage your employees, create a scavenger hunt of questions they have to answer, such as where did your senior partner receive his undergraduate degree? And, when did our Cleveland office open? Have 20 or more questions, and all those who get them correct will be entered into a drawing for dinner for two or other prizes.
- Send a well-designed postcard or nice announcement/envelope announcing the new site. Think ahead, however. Do not be satisfied driving traffic just this once. When you design your mailing, think of ways to get visitors to return a second and third time.
- Undertake an online advertising campaign that drives visitors to specific areas of your site using "vanity URLs" (e.g., www.lawfirmname.com/venturecapital or www.lawfirmname.com/tomjones). Using good web analytics tools, this has the added benefit of measuring how effective your advertising campaign is.
- E-mail the site link to your clients, referral sources, and friends of the firm. Tell them you want their opinions, and keep track of these for future

updates and upgrades. (Be prepared to accept both praise and criticism.) Share these responses with your internal and external web development team.

- It is critical to keep lawyers engaged—staff, too—for months and years after launch. Ensure that your web marketing plan designs fun ways to keep them coming back. This will help ensure that they keep their bios and other content current.

GROWING YOUR SITE

Remember that building a website is an evolving process, not an event. Do not forget about it and assume it will continue to work for you. Your marketing plan should outline how you might expand the scope and reach of your website over its lifetime—assume five years. For example, will you:

1. Translate portions of it into a foreign language?
2. Add an intranet or extranet?
3. Ensure that all lawyers have their social media icons on their bios?
4. Introduce new microsites and blogs, which feed into the home page, bio, and practice pages?
5. Add an advanced search feature, which enables visitors to more easily find what they want?
6. Add other functionality that further engages visitors around signature practice and industry areas, such as video, podcasts, webinars?
7. Leverage your content and regular publishing by ensuring that all alerts, updates, and news items are syndicated on other sites, such as Lexology, JD Supra and your own Twitter, LinkedIn, and Facebook pages?
8. Climb into your analytics and learn what visitors like on your site, how they are accessing it, and from where? Let this dictate where your next investments of time and money should be.
9. Once a year, eliminate pages that are not getting visited? Take them off your site.
10. Freshen your content as frequently as possible? Do so often. Really often. No, seriously, really really often.

Mobile

While there have been numerous changes in how people use the Internet over the past few years, the hardware people use to access the Internet is certainly one of the most important. When the first edition of *The Lawyer's Guide to Marketing on the Internet* was published in 1996, Internet access meant having a personal computer and a bulky cathode ray tube (CRT) monitor that occupied much of a person's desk. By the time the second edition of the book was published a few years later (2002), laptops and larger flat screen monitors were more common and website developers had to begin considering how sites appeared on both larger and smaller screens.

The third edition of this book was released in 2007, just before the debut of the Apple iPhone. But even if the book had been written a few months later, it is doubtful that we would have successfully predicted just how revolutionary that product and the many other amazing phones and tablets would be. Consider the following:

- As of 2014, more than 1.2 billion smartphones had been sold across the world.
- In 2015, 64 percent of Americans had smartphones, up from 35 percent in 2011.
- Eighty-nine percent of smartphone users browse the web or access the Internet on their phones, 88 percent use e-mail, and 75 percent access social media applications.

- Between Android and Apple, nearly 100 billion apps have been down-loaded as of 2014.
- In 2015, Google stated that, for the first time, more than half of all web searches using its website is done on mobile devices versus desktops.

You may even be reading this book on a smartphone or tablet.

The answer to the question of whether it is worth the extra effort to make sure your website is mobile-friendly probably changed in April 2015 when Google announced it was changing its search algorithm based on the way websites ranked when searched from mobile devices (plenty of media buzz around the term "Mobilegeddon"). Google now considers whether a website is mobile-friendly when it ranks sites seen by people searching on a mobile device. Google has indicated that searchers on desktops and tablets are not affected. But given the massive increase in searches on mobile devices, developing a website that is not mobile-friendly is a mistake.

CONTENT STRATEGIES

While it may seem obvious how smartphones and tablets are used, try to make a concerted effort over a few days to observe how you use your devices. Aside from phone calls, how else are you using your phone? Are you using apps that utilize your phone's built in Global Positioning System (GPS) functionality? Are you shopping, texting, accessing social media sites like Facebook, Instagram, or Twitter, consuming news content, answering e-mails, making appointments, etc.? The goal is to broaden the way you are thinking about what content you will deliver to mobile devices.

Obviously, you want to deliver key information about your firm, just as you are doing on your desktop website. That means including lawyer biographies, practice area profiles, and news about the law firm. Feeding in useful content about your area of law is also a way to connect with clients and potential clients. That might mean creating feeds for your social media content. Tweets, blog posts, podcast feeds, and YouTube videos all can be easily incorporated into your mobile site or app.

A mobile site or app should also be programmed to take advantage of the phone's technology. So, add a link that will pull up the phone's mapping app and allow people to get turn-by-turn directions to your office. You can also program a site to automatically dial a phone number when a person taps the number on the web page.

Dorsey's mobile web page packs a lot of information on the screen, but is not so busy that it is tough to navigate. Note that the most common reason a person is

Dorsey's mobile web page

going to a page is to find information on a particular lawyer or general information about the firm—it is easy to navigate to them.

Firms are getting more and more creative in developing content that is specifically designed to take advantage of the features of a phone or tablet. For example, some have incorporated features that:

- Allow clients to see their bills and pay them from their phones
- Allow clients to view case reports in a project management system, such as Basecamp or other web apps
- Provide live chat functionality
- Assist clients and potential clients in keeping track of time lost due to an injury
- Allow clients to view documents in their files via shared Dropbox folders
- Let clients request appointments with lawyers
- Push notifications to the user when important news in the field is breaking

Some firms have developed online calculators for determining child support and calculating the costs of global sourcing. Others are incorporating e-books that can open in the phone's Kindle, iBooks, or Nook browsing software. Another lets the user snap a photo of an accident or other scene and upload the image to the attorney.

Here are a few examples of firms that have developed apps or mobile websites that have innovative content strategies:

1. Pillsbury Crisis Management Toolkit

   Pillsbury's free app provides compelling information and makes it easy to connect with the firm in the case of an emergency.

Pillsbury's free app

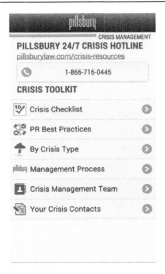

2. Eversheds Sutherland SALT Shaker

   Eversheds Sutherland's SALT Shaker is a resource for all things related to state and local taxation (SALT) issues. The app features a map that the user can zoom with the user's fingers and drill down to find information about tax laws and news in a particular geographic region. The firm allows users to opt in to receive push notifications about developments in the field.

Eversheds Sutherland's SALT Shaker app

3. Constangy, Brooks, Smith and Prophete, LLP

Constangy's Employment Law Resources app is content-rich with guides and checklists on employment law, calculators for workers comp and wage and hour claims, and even a game to entertain clients.

Constangy's Employment Law Resources app

A game from Constangy's Employment Law Resources app

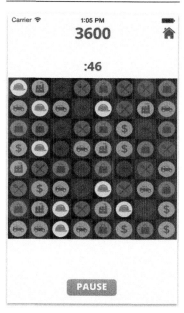

4. Law Offices of Charles D. Naylor

The Law Offices of Charles D. Naylor, a California-based maritime firm, has a longshore injury practice. The firm has developed a highly specialized app called Time Tracker—shown below—that helps clients collect information necessary for their cases.

The specialized Time Tracker app from The Law Offices of Charles D. Naylor

SETTING UP YOUR MOBILE SITE OR APP

After you have settled on a content strategy for your mobile site or app, difficult questions must be answered. One of the most challenging is what type of mobile presence you will seek. There are four major options, namely:

- Native app
- Web app
- Responsive web design (RWD)
- Hybrid design

Native apps are applications that reside on the device and do not necessarily require Internet access to work. The code required for native apps is going to be specific to the device of the user. An app designed for the iPhone will have different source code than one designed for a Windows phone or an Android device. The illustrations for the five firms noted above are all examples of native apps. While some app designers can design for more than one kind of platform, this may not be the case, which can drive up costs and cost you time. Native apps must also be downloaded, which is one more reason someone may decide it is not worth the bother.

Web apps use a mobile device's web browser and can function on any type of smartphone. They do not require downloading, and many have a unique mobile address like "m.yourdomain.com" rather than the typical www.yourdomain.com. The site is designed specifically for mobile devices and tablets, and the coding for the mobile site differs from that on the firm's main site. Be sure to provide a link to the firm's desktop website version since some users may prefer this.

Katten Muchin's web app resembles a native app and has much of the same functionality, without the need for downloading.

Responsive web design sites use coding that detects the type of screen being used. If a phone is being used to access a website, the content will be delivered in a way best seen on a small touchscreen. The same content will be presented differently on a 21-inch monitor.

Winston & Strawn's mobile site is responsive. The left-hand image is seen on an iPhone 6 and the right-hand image is what the same site looks like on a Macbook Pro with a 13-inch screen.

Google has created a handy tool to evaluate whether a website is mobile-friendly or not. The link is at https://www.google.com/webmasters/tools/mobile-friendly/.

Hybrid apps use traditional web coding inside an "app shell" so that it runs like an app instead of a website. These apps can use a one-size-fits all design so it is not necessary to have a completely separate app for each of the major types of devices. Perhaps the best-known hybrid app is the popular ratings app Yelp.

A good website to visit to see examples of best practices and links to many law firms' mobile sites and apps is lawfirmmobile.com.

Katten Muchin's web app

Winston & Strawn's mobile site

Winston & Strawn's desktop site

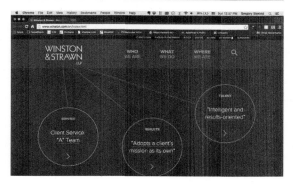

The following chart reviews the major advantages and disadvantages of each type of design. No matter which you choose, each can help establish your presence in an ever-burgeoning marketplace.

ADVANTAGES AND DISADVANTAGES OF MOBILE PLATFORMS

Native App	Web App	Responsive Design	Hybrid A
Advantages			
No internet required	One design	One set of coding for both the regular and mobile site	No Internet required
Graphics are usually better	Much less expensive than an app	One web address for both desktop and mobile versions	One set of coding to get much of native app's functionality
Usually runs faster than websites	Users can get there through search engines or links on social media		Cheaper than a native app developed for each type of device
Can better incorporate phone features, including camera and GPS	Can incorporate some phone features such as phone number dialing via touch and GPS		
Users typically prefer the look of an app to a website	No need to push updates to viewers		
Can better handle features such as personalization and user accounts			
Better integrates touch			
Disadvantages			
Pricier than other options	Graphics and speed slower and inferior to a native app	Can be tricky to convert existing site and optimize for touch and integration with phone features and GPS	Will not have the look of apps designed for a particular device
More time-consuming to design for multiple platforms	Requires Internet	Can end up requiring a major redesign of existing site to achieve the desired functionality on both desktop and mobile	May not run as fast as a native app

Native App	Web App	Responsive Design	Hybrid A
Users have to download from an app store	Vast search engines may be tougher to get noticed in than app store		Users have to download from an app store
Search engines will not see the content	Requires second set of coding (as opposed to responsive design)		Viewers need to manually update
Viewers need to manually update			Search engines will not see content

A natural question is which of these options is the most costly? Native apps will cost the most because each requires custom code. A firm must pay for separate coding for iOS, Android, and Windows. Responsive web design can also be expensive—it may require redesigning a website in order to get the content to adapt to all types of screens. Mobile websites and hybrid apps should be less expensive because you can develop one set of code for each device and should not need to significantly alter an existing website. But those sites require more maintenance time since the content needs to be separately updated.

Another time and financial cost to consider if you go the app route is the need to promote the fact that you have an app. Your app may be found by the search engines included within the iOS, Android, and Windows app stores. But those stores are filled with thousands and thousands of apps that have no ratings and little evidence that anyone has ever downloaded them. Plan on devoting resources to test market and otherwise promote the app.

Erik Mazzone, director of the Center for Practice Management at the North Carolina Bar Association, has a basic rule of thumb in choosing between an app and a mobile-friendly site: If the app does not do something your users will want to avail themselves of at least once a week, just go with a mobile-optimized website. A good rule of thumb.

11

Social Media Marketing

THE BIG PICTURE

In 2007, when the last edition of this book was published, the term "social media" was becoming hot, but much of the attention was on blogging, which was already very popular in the legal community. Twitter was just a few months old. Facebook only became available to the general public a few months beforehand.

Today, blogging is still important, but the other sites mentioned above, as well as several others, have become an important part of the legal marketing discussion. This chapter provides an overview of social media, but is not intended to get in to the weeds regarding how each site works. There are many excellent books on the particular social media sites, including several published by the American Bar Association (ABA) Law Practice Division. Rather, this chapter is intended to provide an overview of the major social media tools, what type of content you should post, and how to have an integrated marketing approach using multiple social media tools together—and also use other Internet and offline marketing tools to promote your social media content (and vice versa).

There is a seeming endless supply of social media sites available to lawyers. You probably have seen groups of icons like this next to online news articles that allow readers to "share" and cross-post an article.

A "share" menu with links to social media sites

There are limits on how much time you have and, since each site works differently, a limit to how many sites you can really master. Also, some social media sites are going to have more potential than others as far as delivering marketing results. Where you choose to spend your social media time should depend on your target audiences and the sites on which they are likely to visit.

Many lawyers make the mistake of assuming that marketing is only about finding new clients. And they are certainly important. But, over time, if you are not getting a lot of referrals from your existing and prior clients, you are doing something wrong. Social media can be a helpful way to stay on their radar screen.

A lot of your new business may be coming from other lawyers who do not practice in your field or lawyers in your field who cannot handle a particular matter—because it is not in their core area of expertise, they are in another geographic area, or because they have a conflict of interest. They may also be in-house counsel—lawyers who frequently use social media sites to research law firms they are evaluating and considering. Becoming known as a thought-leader in a field through your regular postings on social media is a way to get on the short list.

Potential hires will often check out a lawyer or a law firm on social media to learn about the firm's practice and get a sense of its personality. You should assume your professional profiles on sites like LinkedIn are going to be viewed before any potential hire accepts a position.

Perhaps your aim is to get on the radar screen of journalists who write about your field. If you are regularly posting compelling content, a reporter may decide you are the right person to go to for a comment on something about which they are writing.

Finally, government and elected officials are on social media like everyone else. The connections you develop with these folks online may translate to your being able to better resolve problems for your clients, as well as to advocate for better policies.

BLOGS

Blogs (formally known as weblogs) no longer need the same introduction we provided in earlier editions of this book. They have been around since the late 1990s (the first law blog was written by Greg Siskind, co-author of this book) and they are still popular, with the number of law blogs noted in Chapter 3.

Blogging became very popular in a short time because the software made it easy. Web-based blogging tools allowed users to type their blog posts and make edits, much as they were used to doing with e-mail programs and word processing software. Today, many websites themselves are developed using blogging tools like WordPress or Joomla, and the blog has become a hybrid sometimes more closely resembling a website and often seeming closer to other social media tools.

Blogs are not social *networks* like Facebook and Twitter where content is generated by a community of participants and no one person is designated as the person producing the media being discussed. However, they are social media and are designed to foster social *interaction*, particularly in the form of comments from readers. Traditional websites provide media intended simply to be consumed, while blogs are intended to be a part of a two-way communication between the blogger and the blog readers.

We are still including blogging in our discussion of social media tools for several reasons:

- Blogs are updated regularly and are designed to have regular reader followers
- Posts are chronologically organized (the "log" in "blog")
- Blogs are designed to be interactive with readers adding to the discussion in the comments and linking to blog posts in other social media and the blogger providing links from other individuals in the blog post itself
- Blogs tend to be more personal
- Blog content often overlaps with other social media tools with blog posts easily being shared and other social media posts being pulled in to a blog.

There are plenty of examples of excellent law blogs to read for good ideas on how to approach creating your own. The ABA's annually published Blawg 100 (http://www.abajournal.com/blawg100/) is an excellent list of many of the best blogs produced by members of the legal community. Another helpful resource is Justia's BlawgsSearch ("blawg" being the cute nickname for law blogs, and the term "blog" was just a cute nickname for web logs). You can find the site at http://blawgsearch.justia.com/. The site catalogs thousands of law-related blogs by topic and also organizes them by popularity, in addition to having its own search engine. A third useful resource is the book *Blogging in One Hour for Lawyers*, written by Ernie Svenson and published by the ABA's Law Practice Division.

There may now be a lot of competition in social medial for a lawyer's time, but blogs are still one of the best places to devote writing time (as noted earlier in this book, corporate counsel buyers of legal services read blogs and consider them a factor when evaluating counsel). For an individual seeking to establish expertise in a particular area, blogs provide a useful platform and the content can easily be cross-posted on other social media sites. Search engines also look kindly on blog content and often will rank these posts at the beginning of search results.

Justia's BlawgSearch at http://blawgsearch.justia.com/

LINKEDIN

For many lawyers, LinkedIn will be the single most important social media site on which to focus. It is certainly the most popular in the legal community. The site already has 467 million users (more than 128 million of whom are in the United States) and the odds are strong that you have already created at least a minimal profile on the site. LinkedIn is primarily a site for business networking and conversation, as opposed to other social media tools, which people are using in their personal lives as well.

LinkedIn centers on profiles for businesses, individuals, universities, groups, and job opportunities. Individuals' profiles are largely online resumes, while companies' pages are akin to a web page. Thousands of LinkedIn groups allow participants to interact via discussions, postings, and uploading of documents. Like Facebook, Twitter, and other sites, individuals follow each other.

Succeeding with LinkedIn starts with developing a solid LinkedIn profile. This is critical because people are often using LinkedIn as a search engine. The better your profile, the more likely people will find you—and when they do, a well-written profile will increase the likelihood they will reach out to contact you.

LinkedIn's feature-set is extensive and the site is not always as intuitive to navigate as it should be. While this chapter is intended to give you a sense of how LinkedIn might fit in to your marketing, the ABA Law Practice Division book *LinkedIn in One Hour for Lawyers*, Second Edition, by Dennis Kennedy and Allison Shields, is well worth reading for a more in-depth treatment.

A LinkedIn Profile

Setting up a LinkedIn profile is fairly straightforward and mainly involves filling out a series of short forms. Sections of your profile include the following:

- The headline
- Summary
- Contact information
- Posts
- Awards and honors
- Graphics
- Education
- Experience
- Projects/cases
- Publications
- Languages
- Pro bono/volunteer work
- Linked documents

The headline and summary sections of the profile are critical and often left out when people create their profiles. When you search LinkedIn and a list of individual profiles is shown, the individual's name is accompanied by the headline the person created, thus making it easier for people to quickly scan the results to find the person they are looking for. The headline is where you should state your title and area of specialization. Some people try to be cute or clever with their headlines, but if it is not clear from the headline what you do, you are going to lose people. In the contact details below your website, you have the option to include up to three web addresses. Take advantage to share important links and fill out all three. For example, include your law firm's web page, your blog address, and your biography page. You can also include an instant messaging address for a service like Skype or Yahoo! Messenger, as well as your Twitter address.

A section of the author's LinkedIn profile in editing mode

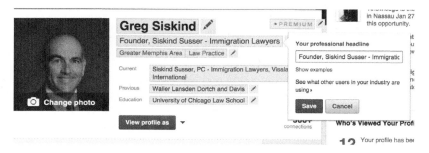

Each line of the profile as well as the photograph can be individually edited and LinkedIn offers examples of what might be included.

The summary shows up just under the headers. It is a free form section that allows you to quickly introduce yourself. It is really the equivalent of your 15 second "elevator speech," so you will want to list the most important things about yourself in the summary and then you can expand on them in later sections of your profile.

The headers also include a photograph. Not including one is a big mistake—people will wonder why you did not post one. But, avoid posting a picture that is not "professional" or one from 20 years ago. Your photo should be full-frame, in color, recent, have a clear resolution, and show a pleasant expression (as opposed to an overly serious scowl or a full smile). If you are expecting people to accept your connection request, make a good first impression with your photo.

Many lawyers will fill in just the most basic information—colleges attended and prior jobs. But keep revisiting your profile and focus on filling in as many sections as you can.

Joshua Lipp's LinkedIn profile

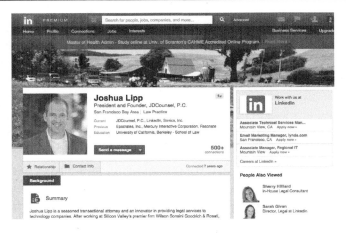

Attorney Joshua Lipp has his own company as well as working for LinkedIn's in-house legal department. Josh takes advantage of the feature that allows you to have a background image behind your profile, in this case an image of a rare part of Silicon Valley without a technology company headquarters.

Skills, Endorsements, and Recommendations

LinkedIn allows you to add specific skills to your profile. Within your practice area, you will likely find a number of specific types of specializations and skill sets that apply. For example, within immigration law, there are skill listings for many types of visa petitions. If you do not select skills, LinkedIn will sometimes select keywords from your profile. This is hardly a perfect system and the skills selected on your behalf may not be a very close match. If you use this feature, be sure to carefully select skills that actually match your background.

When you log in to LinkedIn and view a profile, you will see a grouping of four of your connections asking if you wish to endorse any of them for a particular skill. The skills that show up matching for a particular connection will be one of the first ten the individual has in their particular profile. Your connections will see you show up for endorsing in one of the skills on your list and can endorse you with one click.

Your connections can also write recommendations on your behalf. These are free-form testimonials written by your connections.

The skills, endorsements, and recommendations features can all be turned off and some may choose to do this if their state's ethics rules bar them. Before you seek or accept these endorsements and recommendations, fully understand your state's ethics rules. Further discussion of the ethics implications of features like this is contained in Chapter 17.

Groups

Aside from building your resume and making connections, LinkedIn also has thousands of online groups that allow people to engage in discussions and read content on topics of interest. From a marketing perspective, becoming active in a LinkedIn group is a way to present yourself as a thought leader in your field—and learn from other respected colleagues—even people you do not know. To find groups, go to "Interests" on LinkedIn's menu, click on "Groups," and then you will land on a page where you can search for groups. Groups can be good places for lawyers to post content, answer questions (within the bounds of ethical constraints), and keep up on developments in clients' industries. Some groups are open to everyone and others require you to be accepted by the group's moderator. Once you are admitted in to a group, you can begin a discussion or join in one already started. You can also see which of your connections are members of the group. Prior discussions are searchable from this page as well.

If there is no group on the topic most of interest, you can also start a group of your own. By doing so and serving as moderator, you can get to know the group's members and have some credibility as an issue expert since you are the creator of the group and no doubt one of its major contributors.

Law Firm Pages

Be sure to create a separate LinkedIn page for your law firm. On the page, again, enter as much information in your firm's profile as you can and add your firm's logo. You should add your firm's areas of specialization. Like a lawyer's individual profile, include keywords wherever possible. Not sure what keywords to use? Browse the selection at Google Adwords (adwords.google.com).

Once you have created your firm's LinkedIn page, ask the firm's lawyers and staff to add the firm's page to their profiles and then ask each person to change their profile page so the new firm page shows up on their individual pages. You can also ask clients and others to post recommendations (again, following your state's ethics rules). As with your firm's website, you can post updates and add links.

One final tip—LinkedIn's feature of automatically notifying your connections when you make changes to your profile is irritating. Turn that feature off.

Publishing

LinkedIn has been emerging as an importing publishing platform in the past few years. LinkedIn Pulse is, in essence, a news feed aggregating site within LinkedIn. It pulls featured articles by well-known individuals and also pulls in articles written on Pulse's writing tool by the LinkedIn member's connections. Pulse's main page is curated so you are not likely going to end up on the main page, but your post will show up in LinkedIn's internal search engine. You can also post short updates and links to other locations using LinkedIn's status update feature (similar to other social media sites like Facebook, Pulse can be found in a dropdown list under "Interests" in LinkedIn's menu bar).

Pulse's writing tool on LinkedIn

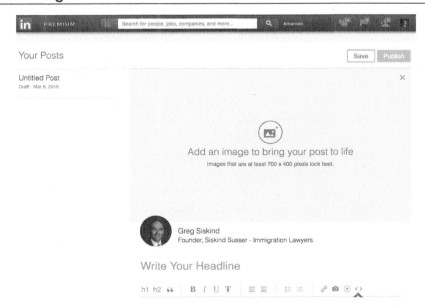

LinkedIn acquired SlideShare in 2012 and greatly expanded its publishing platform. SlideShare is a tool that allows for the sharing of presentation slides as well as other documents. In addition to being a useful place to gain exposure for your writing, presentations uploaded to SlideShare can be embedded in your blog and website. Like Pulse, Slideshare can be found under "Interests" in LinkedIn's menu bar.

A presentation in SlideShare

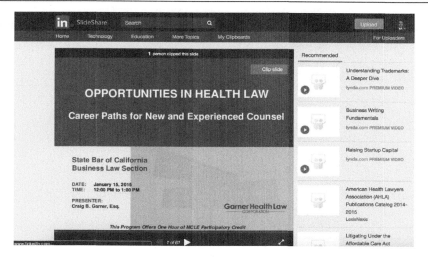

Keep in mind you will need to post regularly if you expect to see results. Like a Facebook or Twitter feed, a lot of your connections will miss your posts because they are not checking often and are following too many people.

ProFinder

LinkedIn recently added a new directory of professional service providers that includes a section for lawyers. The service is free for both the provider and the person shopping for the service professional. Individuals seeking a lawyer can submit a request for a proposal and will receive up to five quotes from people selected based on the LinkedIn profile. The process for submitting your name for inclusion in ProFinder is very simple. LinkedIn screens providers, though it is not clear what criteria are used to determine who will and will not be included.

Connections

LinkedIn will deliver a lot more results as the number of your connections expands. But how can you fortify your connections with people you actually want in your network? First, LinkedIn has a tool to check your contacts list to see which people are already in LinkedIn. You can send invitations out to as many of those individuals as appropriate (i.e., consistent with your ethics rules regarding solicitations, as well as to people you genuinely want in your network), and you can also have LinkedIn regularly checking to let you know when people on your existing contact list join the network. You can also invite people on your contact list without LinkedIn accounts to join, but some might find this annoying—be careful before sending out these requests.

Add people you are meeting in the course of your work, especially your existing clients. When you get a new business card, instead of just sending an e-mail follow up, connect with the person on LinkedIn and send your follow up note in the text of the LinkedIn invitation. And add potential referral sources like lawyers at other firms who refer work to you (and vice versa). You can also connect with reporters who cover your practice area or whom you have dealt with in the past.

A LinkedIn invitation

✉ Invite **Marcine** to connect on LinkedIn

How do you know Marcine?
○ Colleague
○ Classmate
○ We've done business together
○ Friend
● Other

Marcine's email address:

○ I don't know Marcine

Include a personal note: (optional)

Hi Marcine - Nice meeting you at the conference this week.

- Greg Siskind

[Send Invitation] or Cancel

If you use Evernote, the mobile app for iPhones and Android devices has a clever feature that allows you to photograph a business card, have all the data transcribed into a contact on your phone (and add it to Outlook as well), and then send a connection invitation to the person on LinkedIn.

A contact in the Evernote mobile app

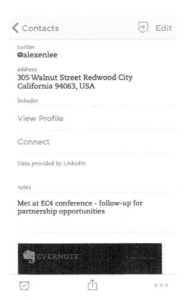

‹ Contacts   ⬚ Edit

twitter
@alexenlee

address
**305 Walnut Street Redwood City
California 94063, USA**

linkedin

View Profile

Connect

Data provided by LinkedIn

notes

**Met at EC4 conference - follow-up for
partnership opportunities**

EVERNOTE

☑   ⬆   ○ ○ ○

LinkedIn makes it easy to invite people who you may know but who are not in your contacts directory. LinkedIn divides the world into four groups:

- 1st connections—Individuals who are already your connections
- 2nd connections—Individuals who are connected to your 1st connections
- Group members—Individuals who are members of the same groups as you
- 3rd + everyone else—Individuals who are connected to your 2nd connections plus everyone else on LinkedIn.

LinkedIn will regularly send you suggested connections. On the LinkedIn website, you can go to the page "People You May Know," which will display snapshot profiles for people with whom you have common connections or interests. You are likely to find people you know on that page.

Devote time each week to invite people to connect with you. Consider adding your LinkedIn address on your business card. Many people do not know that after you have 25 connections, LinkedIn allows you to switch from your original profile address—a complicated combination of letters and numbers—to one that is much simpler, such as www.linkedin.com/in/johndoe.

Even if you are not adding connections, LinkedIn is a great way to learn more about your clients and prospective clients. You can review a lot of very helpful information on the backgrounds of people in those organizations, and about the organizations themselves through the companies' pages. And when your contact at a client changes companies, which you will know if you review your LinkedIn notifications page or have your LinkedIn profile configured to send you e-mails when your connections change positions, you can easily stay in touch with the contact and stay on the radar screen to provide legal services to the new organization. Even if you do not see an initial notification that a connection has changed positions, it is good to check the person's LinkedIn profile if you have not been in touch in a while.

Finally, do not forget to fill out the "Relationship" section of a person's profile. One feature that is not widely known but can be very helpful in your marketing is assigning tags to your contacts. You can create custom tags that allow you to categorize your connections. Then you can search based on those categories and also send e-mails to that tagged group of connections. For example, say you create a tag for your clients in a particular industry. You might want to send out an e-mail

Using tags on LinkedIn

via LinkedIn letting them know of an important development in their industry. You can assign and create tags easily from within the relationship section of a profile.

You can also include notes about how you met the person (lest you wonder years later to whom the unfamiliar face belongs) and set reminders to follow up with the person at a later time.

Profile Views

One of the more intriguing aspects of LinkedIn is the feature that allows you to not only see statistics on how many people are viewing your profile, but the names and profiles of the individual people who have visited. It is possible to turn on a privacy setting that keeps the person viewing a profile anonymous, though most people either do not care or do not know to turn the feature off. LinkedIn apparently thinks it is good for people to know you have visited their profile page.

But there are lots of instances where that might not be so wise. For example, if you are doing market research and are looking at a competitor's page, do you really want to advertise that. Or perhaps you are shopping for services from someone and you do not want to be contacted by them for a sales call. Or you are a litigator researching a potential juror and you are concerned about the juror seeing that you viewed their profile lest it be considered an impermissible communication.

In short, there are too many examples of where having this feature turned on can cause you headaches. Checking the data on this page from time to time can show if you are making progress in increasing the visibility of your page.

Building Relationships

Simply collecting connections on LinkedIn and doing nothing further is better than nothing, but you are wasting an opportunity. Building relationships is the name of the game. When your connections add accomplishments to their LinkedIn pages, it is a nice excuse to reach out to them. When they post articles and news, you can "like" them and comment as well. When you are visiting a city on a business trip, do a search on LinkedIn and pull up all your connections in the place you are

The Advanced People Search feature on LinkedIn

visiting (even narrowed down to a zip code and radius) and make a point of sched-
uling visits. LinkedIn makes it easy to filter your connections geographically.

Search Engine Optimization (SEO)

One of the most important considerations when completing your profile is optimizing search engine results. This would include search engines like Google and Bing,
as well as LinkedIn's own internal search engine. There are a number of ways to
improve the chances that your profile will come up high in the results list, such as:

- Fully complete your profile. This increases the likelihood that terms about
  you will come up in a search. Also, once you set up a LinkedIn profile, you
  are likely to find that Google will rank your profile near the top of a search
  of your name (such as might happen when a prospective client is checking you out). Yet another reason to ensure that your profile is "ready for
  prime time."
- List all of your relevant skills, since people may be searching by those
  terms.
- Be thoughtful about including keywords throughout your profile, including in the headers. For example, instead of saying Partner at Smith and
  Brown, say "Intellectual Property Litigation Partner at Smith and Brown,
  Attorneys at Law."
- Join groups relevant to your practice areas and skills. The group name
  will be picked up by search engines, which may get your profile additional
  attention.
- Add connections (though not irrelevant ones). LinkedIn's search engine
  will elevate 1st and 2nd degree connections, so the more people you have
  in common, the more likely you will rank high in a search inquiry.

LinkedIn Premium

LinkedIn has a free version used by most people and it has various premium services available at prices between $20 and $75 per month. Some of the premium
features are aimed at job seekers and recruiters. But others are aimed at power
users of LinkedIn, who are interested in expanding their access to certain features.
For example, premium users get a certain number of InMail messages (the number
varies from three to 30 per month depending on what premium plan you choose),
which allow you to e-mail anyone on LinkedIn even if the person is not one of your
connections.

Premium users can see the full list of everyone who has viewed their profiles
in the prior three months if the viewers have not changed their privacy setting
to anonymous or totally anonymous. Free users can only see the last five people. They can also view analytics on their profile, including what search terms
turned up their profiles and a breakdown geographically of where their pages' visitors come from. Premium subscribers can search using more filters, such as the

person's function, company size, years of experience, and what LinkedIn groups they have joined, when hunting for connections, and those searches can be saved and set up for notifications when new connections are added to the results. Finally, LinkedIn will limit the number of 3rd connection profiles you can view unless you pay for a premium subscription.

LinkedIn's free services are certainly excellent and may be fine for most. But as you get more experienced with the social network, you may want to upgrade.

TWITTER

From a technical standpoint, Twitter is probably the easiest social media tool to master. After all, you just need to be able to type a 140-character message. Well, there is a little more to it, but there are not that many additional things to know. Nevertheless, while it is easy to tweet, it is also easy to be lousy at it.

There are some good places to go for starters when you are ready to dip your toes in to the Twitter pond. Justia's Legal Birds page provides an extensive directory of lawyers using Twitter that is broken up by area of specialization as well as the size of their audience.

Justia's Legal Birds page

You can also pick up a lot of helpful information in the ABA Law Practice Division book *Twitter in One Hour for Lawyers*, by Jared Correia.

Take time to carefully construct your Twitter profile. First, you need to choose a username. You can try for your name, but be prepared for it to be taken—there were more than 300 million Twitter users as of the writing of this chapter. You can also do some kind of combination of your name and profession (e.g., johnsmithesq).

Some choose to have both personal and professional Twitter accounts. But keep in mind that everything on Twitter is public, so trying to separate the two is not so easy. And some of the best and most interesting lawyer Twitter users blend the personal and work-related content.

Twitter allows you to make your Tweets private to only your followers. That may be fine if your goal is to communicate with your clients and colleagues, but if the goal is to get a solid marketing benefit, then keep your Twitter feed public. When you are configuring your account, you can also choose to get e-mail notifications of when people send you messages, mention your Twitter username in a tweet, retweet one of your tweets, follow you, or favorite one of your tweets. We recommend that you opt to receive e-mails at the beginning so that you are regularly reminded to log back in. After you have a number of followers and are posting regularly, you will probably get sick of all the e-mails and may just want to turn off that feature.

Next step is to create your profile. It is not nearly as involved as creating your LinkedIn profile, but you will want to choose a photo to upload since Twitter will otherwise assign you an avatar (typically an egg on a colored background). Most people (wisely) choose to load a professional looking headshot, though people can get pretty creative here. But often what one person considers creative, another considers silly or weird.

Then, insert a biography in just 160 characters. Jared Correia, author of the ABA book *Twitter in One Hour for Lawyers*, says the bio "is the equivalent of your Twitter elevator speech, a short-form pitch . . ., before the person looking at your profile sees any of your tweets. Just as with an elevator speech, your hearer knows nothing, as yet, of your bone fides or of your specific experience."

You can also add a background design. You can go minimal and just add a color behind your bio and next to your photo. Or you can choose an image as wallpaper. The background image you choose can show a little more creativity than your headshot.

Once your account is set up, you are ready to go. Here are some basics you will need to know. First, you can send "direct messages" to people who follow you. These are private messages, though novices have made the mistake of thinking they were sending a direct message and then ended up posting for all the world to see. Approach this with caution!

Tweets need to be fewer than 140 characters. After a while, you will get smarter about how to pack a lot in to a tweet. Go to a site like https://bitly.com/ or TinyURL.com and you can have web links you are posting shortened to just a few characters. People on Twitter use shorthand to save space like saying B4 rather than "before," OTOH for "on the other hand," etc. If you cannot squeeze it in to one post, you can divide it up into multiple tweets each ending with something like 1/2, 2/2, pt. 3, and so on. And when you have multiple parts, consider posting as replies to the initial tweet rather than sending each part as a completely new tweet. This will make it easier for the reader to find and quickly read the various parts together.

If you type a person's Twitter username preceded by ",," the person will be notified that they have been mentioned in your tweet, which can be helpful if you are trying to bring them in to a conversation or just want to give them a hat tip that something they have said or done is worth noting. If you add a hashtag (#) and then follow it with a particular keyword, people searching that hashtag will find your tweet along with all other tweets with the same hashtag.

You can retweet other tweets you like and many people add the letters RT in front to make it clear the words are someone else's tweet. You can either retweet it in its entirety, modify it (usually putting MT at the front to indicate it is a modified tweet), or click "Quote Tweet," which allows you to type a new 140-character tweet and show the retweeted message in a smaller font set off slightly in a box below your text.

And you can "like" tweets by clicking on the heart underneath the tweet. The author of the tweet will be notified. Sometimes you simply want to let the person who posted a tweet know that you appreciate what they have stated, but are not interested in sharing that with all of your followers. Retweeting a message, on the other hand, ensures that all of your followers will see the original tweet. If you do not think the tweet is going to be of interest to the rest of your followers, the "like" option is useful.

Like other social media, if you post compelling content, you will develop a following and gain credibility as an expert. Some people try to game the system by buying followers or following as many people as possible and hoping they will be followed back in return. Either is a pretty bad idea. It may take a while, but if you post solid content, participate in conversations on Twitter by providing useful comments, and follow people whom you actually want to follow because of what they have to say, people will start following you in return. And when people retweet your comments, they will be exposing their network of followers to you.

You can also gain followers by simply telling people you already know that you are on Twitter. Include your Twitter username in your marketing materials and in your e-mail signature block, let your Facebook friends know you are on Twitter, and search out your friends on Twitter and follow them. But remember that the number of Twitter followers you have is less important than who you have following you and why. Are they clients and potential clients, potential referral sources, reporters, and others who follow you because you have interesting and important things to say? Or are they people who follow you along with thousands of others and are not really paying attention.

You also will want to commit to posting regularly if you want to develop a following. Post a few tweets a day and retweet a few tweets and reply to other people's tweets. You do not need to spend a lot of time on Twitter to get this done.

When you are new to Twitter, figuring out whom to follow can be a challenge. Here is a short list of people to consider:

- Thought leaders in your field of law
- Bar organizations of which you are a member, as well as other organizations that might generate content of interest to you
- Reporters and pundits who cover your field
- Fellow lawyers who have large followings to provide examples of how to engage on Twitter and what people find interesting.

- If you are engaged in advocacy, follow people who represent views opposing yours, and those who support your view. Note that following someone is not an endorsement of their views.
- Those who are tweeting about subjects of personal interest—public figures, those with similar hobby interests, etc.

In some instances, you will be tempted to follow people simply because they are following you. You may see this as being polite, but it can quickly get unwieldy. Only follow people you are genuinely interested in hearing from.

After you are following a large number of people, you may want to start using Twitter lists. You can group your followers according to various categories such as people in your professional and community organizations, your town, reporters and news media, colleagues, etc. Setting up a Twitter list is pretty easy. Go to twitter.com/lists and click on the button "create new list." You can make that list public or private. You may be interested in making your list a form of content by letting people know who you think is worth following on a particular subject. After you add a description of the list and hit save, you can add people by clicking on the gear icon drop down menu on the user's profile page. Select "add or remove from lists" and then select the list on which you would like to include the person. You can view tweets from your list by clicking on the lists tab on your profile page and selecting a list. Lists will become more and more important if you let the overall number of people you are following go up. Also, if you are particularly interested in not missing tweets from a group of people, it is easier to stay caught up if you use lists.

Another way to keep your Twitter feed better organized is to use a software product like Tweetdeck (www.tweetdeck.twitter.com), which lets you build custom timelines based on searches and hashtags, your lists, activity on your account, your direct messages, and more.

A Tweetdeck dashboard

Above is a Tweetdeck dashboard showing an example of how you can filter out your Twitter messages by subject, your notifications (when you are mentioned in a tweet or are followed by someone), as well as your overall Twitter feed.

FACEBOOK

When Facebook was new and growing quickly, many businesses created accounts as individual users and "friended" people in the way that is now ubiquitous for most of us. This was a rather clunky way for businesses to operate and Facebook eventually came up with a different solution—creating Facebook pages for businesses and organizations. Similar to websites, Facebook pages allow businesses to interact with the public by posting links to blog and website content, sharing other content, allowing readers to comment, publicizing events, and direct messaging with individuals.

Facebook makes setting up a business page quite easy. While the interface and steps change from time to time, Facebook posts easy-to-follow videos (like the one at https://www.facebook.com/business/learn/set-up-facebook-page) that demonstrate how a page can be created without much in the way of technical skill.

Because Facebook pages have a tightly controlled layout and feature set, law firms will not be able to make their pages look terribly different from one another. But some personalization is possible. You can post a cover image (the banner at the top of the page) and a profile image (often a firm's logo or a picture of the individual attorney running the page). Some firms post pictures of their buildings, their team members, graphics with a tagline, etc. as their cover images. Be sure to use a high quality image for each of these.

Wilson Sonsini's Facebook page

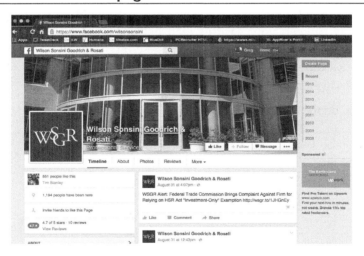

Silicon Valley-based Wilson Sonsini shows off its distinctive headquarters building along with its logo on its Facebook page.

Facebook also offers dozens of settings that can be customized by a business. Many choose to accept the default settings, but it pays to go through them one by one. For example, do you want to allow profanity on your page? Do you want visitors to your site to be able to post to your timeline like they can on a personal Facebook page?

As for what to post to your Facebook page, there is no one size fits all formula. However, Facebook in general has a less formal culture than, say, LinkedIn. The better law firm Facebook pages blend a mix of informative content, posts about firm events, accomplishments, mentions in the news, etc. But they also post about what members of the firm are doing in their personal lives and in the community.

Create a policy around all your social media commitments, which outlines do's and don'ts. Active stewardship is a requirement to get the most benefit out each social media outlet.

Fenwick & West's Facebook page

San Francisco's Fenwick & West's Facebook page featured a photo of dozens of firm employees enjoying the San Francisco Pride Parade and also had a post about pro bono work by a firm attorney.

Firms can also use Facebook to promote their events, set up a documents repository, embed video, and chat in real time with people visiting the page.

Facebook will assign a page URL/address—it will be long and unmemorable. Once you have 25 followers on your page, you can create a custom address—www .facebook.com/mygreatfirm/, for example.

Facebook promotes the purchase of ads to draw visitors to a business page. If you choose to advertise and have researched your ethics rules to ensure you are complying, Facebook has interesting data tools available, including Audience Insights, which allow you to target to a fairly narrow audience (e.g., an elder law attorney might be interested in people over the age of 65 in Miami who earn more than X dollars).

When you post a really compelling post on Facebook—perhaps a link to an important article you have just written—you can "pin" it to the top of your timeline so that it will continue to be seen first by visitors even after you have added additional posts.

How do you get visitors to your firm's Facebook page? The easiest place to start is by asking people in your firm to add a post to their personal Facebook pages asking their friends to visit and "like" the firm's page. You can also publicize your page with clients by including a mention of it in your newsletters, invoices, brochures, etc., saying, "For the latest information on XYZ law and updates on news from Smith Jones & Hanson, please visit our Facebook page at www .facebook.com/smithjoneshanson." And you and your colleagues can include a link to your Facebook page in your e-mail signature block, as well as link on your firm website.

Facebook allows you to pay to boost a post or promote a page. If you are interested in making sure that a particular post reaches the individuals who have liked your law firm's Facebook page, you can pay to "boost" the post and ensure it is seen in the feeds of those people. Because most people have too many Facebook friends and too many liked pages to see everything, Facebook filters out what the user sees and the only way to guarantee people see something is by boosting it. You can also promote your Facebook page on the page of friends of those who have liked your page. The latter is probably lawyer advertising and will have to meet your state's rules. But is "boosting" a post advertising? If someone likes your Facebook page, it might be analogous to subscribing to a law firm newsletter since the person is consenting to receive your content. Boosting is arguably just paying to make sure the requested message is delivered.

Facebook, like Google, offers analytics to help you better understand whether what you are paying delivered for you. But the same questions apply here as in any other form of advertising regarding whether you are getting a good return on your investment and whether you feel comfortable advertising. Content marketing is far less controversial and does not come with the complex set of regulatory requirements.

GOOGLE+

Google+ launched in 2011 and is the company's third foray into developing a social media platform. Google+ has features similar to other social media networks, including allowing businesses to create their own pages for followers and "circles" of individuals in the same social network, using hashtags to get more visibility in searches within Google+, etc. While the number of lawyers and others using Google+ is not as large as some of the other networks discussed in this chapter, there are some important reasons to add Google+ to your social media mix.

First, putting content out on Google+ could help you in your efforts to improve your Google search engine performance. While you may not be seen directly by as many people on Google+, your posted content still can be seen by other networks—simply because you will appear in search results, which include Google+. Second, Google+ is a critical part of Google's local search product. When people

The author's **Google+** page

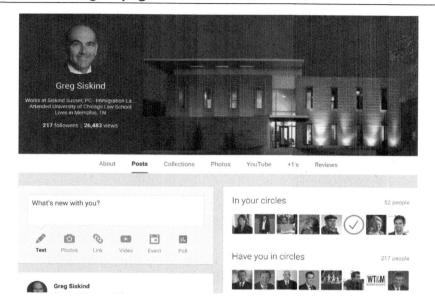

search Google for local lawyers in your field and your name comes up, you can have your Google+ business profile show up on Google, which gives helpful information about your business (directions, phone number, etc.) instead of people having to go hunt the information down on your website. People can also post reviews of you as well, which can benefit you if your satisfied clients post about their experiences. But—be aware of your state bar's rules about client testimonials. Several states prohibit use of these.

Like other sites discussed, the best thing you can do if you use Google+ is to completely fill out your profile. Posting and communicating with others is also important. But you should spend most of your energy on your local Google+ page for your law firm. People are going to search for you in Google, and not taking advantage of this free product could be viewed as marketing malpractice.

AVVO

Avvo is a social media site that most lawyers know, though many have only paid cursory attention. We advise that you get more familiar with it and focus on your profile there. Avvo is a lawyer directory, as well as a site that "rates" lawyers and allows users to post reviews. Lawyers can also post articles and answer reader questions. There are mixed views and reviews of Avvo—both its usefulness and credibility. You will need to evaluate it and decide the investment you want to make. Some lawyers are also now using Avvo to search for lawyers to whom they would like to refer a matter much as they would with a directory like Martindale Hubbell.

Sheila Hahn's Avvo page

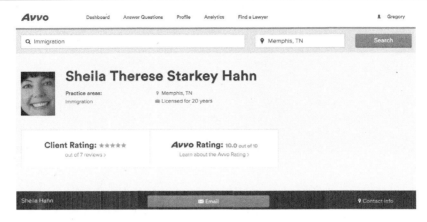

Memphis immigration lawyer Sheila Hahn has a top rating from clients who have reviewed her work as well as a perfect Avvo rating based on a variety of factors discussed below.

Avvo is similar to LinkedIn when it comes to the type of information lawyers can post—background, including academic and employment history, publications, awards, and major cases argued.

> *Even if you have not created an Avvo listing, Avvo may have created a profile for you by pulling data that is publicly available. This is one of the more controversial aspects of Avvo from a lawyer's perspective.*

Note: even if you have not created an Avvo listing, Avvo may have created a profile for you by pulling data that is publicly available. This is one of the more controversial aspects of Avvo from a lawyer's perspective. Avvo does not allow lawyers to delete their profiles because they are available through public records. Many lawyers correct inaccuracies on their profile by "claiming" their profile, which allows the attorney to update the details. However, once the attorney claims the page, Avvo does not allow the person to "unclaim" it. If you do not want to claim your profile, but also do not want inaccurate information showing up, Avvo also states that they will correct the profile upon request. You can e-mail customercare@avvo.com for help with this.

Assuming you want to use Avvo, then focus on your Avvo ratings. Avvo rates attorneys on a scale of 1 to 10 based on a variety of factors including bar leadership positions, publications, awards, speaking engagements, and other factors that the attorney can add in the profile. Avvo also looks at peer endorsements, client reviews (akin to sites like TripAdvisor and Yelp), whether the attorney has added a photo, and whether the attorney has answered client questions in the Avvo question and answer (Q&A) forum. This is obviously a lot different than the peer review process familiar to lawyers who have participated in ratings systems like Chambers, Martindale, and Best Lawyers.

Whether you think this is not as valid as the more familiar and traditional ratings systems, the reality is that Avvo is now a massive site and it is the dominant player in the field. Yelp offers lawyer reviews, but is not widely used by consumers for researching lawyers. The one major potential competitor is Google, which does have a ratings system and is the major source of traffic for Avvo. Avvo is now large enough that it has begun advertising heavily and its brand recognition is growing. Google could potentially become a major competitor for Avvo in the future, but for now, the odds are decent that potential clients will find you on Avvo, and you should carefully consider how best to present yourself to that audience.

It is possible to get a high score on Avvo without having to post content or answer questions. Your book author, Greg Siskind, has managed to obtain a score of 10 without having to seek client endorsements. Avvo does require peer reviews from other attorneys, however, to achieve a top score.

Avvo has an extremely busy Q&A section and many lawyers are answering questions on thousands of topics across most practice areas. Lawyers answering questions from people in online forums has been a feature of the Internet for two decades and it is clearly here to stay. But there are obvious issues with respect to professional conduct rules (see Chapter 17 for more information on this) and lawyers should be cautious and comply with their state's bar rules.

There is also a question of whether it is really worth the time or not. Many questions are answered by multiple lawyers, and it is probable that many questioners do not ultimately hire a lawyer (or are just second-guessing their existing counsel). On the other hand, posting content either in the form of articles or answering questions is a way for people viewing your listing to get a sense about your expertise and, generally, how you think.

Avvo itself has become a search engine. It will often pop up at the top of a Google search for a particular type of attorney in a particular location. And once in Avvo, the site will produce a list of attorneys. The two ways to get to the top of that list are to have a lot of reviews or to pay for Avvo to list you in its sponsored listing (similar to Google's approach of listing advertisers at the top of a search). While the scope of this book is not to discuss advertising strategies, if you are going to pay for a sponsored listing, you have the ability to customize your header and should think about what will be both effective and ethical.

Aside from Avvo's advertising feature, they also offer a paid service called Avvo Pro, which allows lawyers to add more personalization to their profiles, such as removing competitor's ads from their listings, highlighting preferred client reviews, and tracking analytics on their profiles.

Of course, Avvo is known for its consumer ratings system. Lawyers should first see what is already posted about them. If you have a review, and it is negative, you are allowed to post a response. But tread very carefully here. First, you still have ethical obligations regarding client confidentiality, so you cannot specifically address what is being said. A brief response offering an apology is sometimes appropriate. You can also offer to discuss the matter offline with the review writer. If the writer is truly off base, you could say that confidentiality rules prevent a public response, but note that your view of the situation is very different from your reviewer's. You can also contact Avvo if you believe the review is fake—Avvo does have a process to take it down if it believes it is posted by a non-client. If the reviewer is a real client, Avvo will fight attempts to get at the identity of the writer or force the client to remove or alter the review.

If you do get good reviews and want to promote them on your website, consult your state's ethics rules regarding whether this is permissible. As we have noted earlier, certain state bars prohibit including testimonials in your marketing.

> *As you can see from the illustration below, headers like "building a better foundation" or "experienced bankruptcy and foreclosure attorney" convey marketing messages. The words should be carefully considered to ensure compliance with your jurisdiction's ethics rules.*

Search results on Avvo

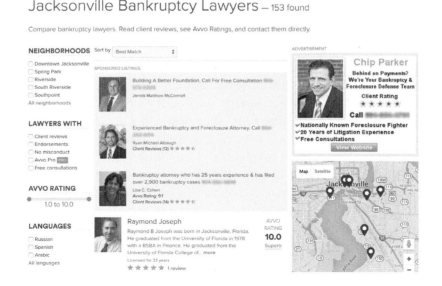

Avvo also has a sponsored listings feature for lawyers interested in ensuring that their profiles are seen at the top of a page. In larger, busier markets, you will be put in a rotation rather than your profile always being seen at the top of each search. Keep in mind that advertising rules for lawyers in your state may come into play as far as limits on what can be said. As for whether there is a sufficient return on investment, like Facebook and Google advertising costs, you can view traffic information to see whether people clicked through and viewed your profile and determine whether those click throughs turned in to actual clients.

OTHER LAWYER SOCIAL MEDIA SITES

JDSupra (www.jdsupra.com) is an example of a social media site aimed at the lawyer community and not the general public. The site is a publishing platform and allows lawyers who blog or write articles another vehicle to extend their reach to their peers The site also invites reporters to submit requests to talk to lawyers and JDSupra plays matchmaker to connect its member lawyers to the press. If your practice depends on getting referral work from other lawyers in the field, you may want to spend time and money on a site like this. Lexology (www .lexology.com) is another publishing site that helps lawyers leverage their articles and presentations.

Martindale-Hubbell Connected (http://community.martindale.com/SignIn.aspx) is LexisNexis's social networking site just for lawyers. The site bills itself as a place for lawyers seeking a rich professional discussion environment in its various message boards. This site will also repost lawyer blog articles. The site differs from JDSupra and Lexology in keeping its focus just to lawyers and not members of the public. From a marketing standpoint, the goal is to develop your referral network within the legal community.

SOCIAL MEDIA MANAGEMENT

One of the biggest challenges you will face when fully exploiting social media is efficiently managing several tools at once—it can be very time consuming. Consider social media management systems, which help you monitor your various accounts and post to multiple sites at one time. They can also monitor social media to see what people are saying about you or your firm. Two of the more popular tools for social media management are Hootsuite (www.hootsuite.com) and Social Defender (www.socialdefender.com). Both also provide analytics on your social media activity. Keep in mind that neither site works with all social networks. But they cover the major ones like Twitter, LinkedIn, Facebook, and Google+.

An example of a Hootsuite page

Hootsuite's social media management system allows for monitoring and posting to multiple social media feeds simultaneously.

SOCIAL MEDIA CONTENT STRATEGIES

Deciding to use social media and learning the ins and outs of the different tools is just the beginning. The next step is to determine what you are actually going to post on these different sites. At the most basic level, you should fully complete your profiles on sites like LinkedIn and Avvo, so that people searching these sites for lawyers in your specialty and geography find you. But if you are looking to produce content on social media, here are a few ideas to successfully engage with your audience:

1. *Be a newscaster*

    Even if you do not have time to do a lot of original writing, you are surely keeping up with developments in your field and in the news generally, which may be important to your clients and referral sources. Simply posting the link to a news article, an interesting case, an article written by another lawyer, or a new regulation or piece of legislation along with a few words describing why the news is important will help establish you as a resource in your field.

2. *Use social media as part of your advocacy marketing strategy*

    Advocating on behalf of your clients by promoting changing laws and regulations is a great way to promote your practice. And it gives you great satisfaction when you are helping to effect change. Social media is a great way to channel those efforts and get out your advocacy message. Follow pundits and journalists covering the beat where you are advocating, activists in your field, legislators pushing relevant bills, lobbyists working on your issues, and certainly opponents of your issues. Your goal is to get a regular stream of information so that you are thoroughly informed. Add comments and repost those posts that further your cause.

3. *Use social media to help out the organizations and clients you serve*

Most lawyers are active in various associations such as bar organizations, chambers of commerce, and non-profits that serve their communities. And many of those organizations rely on social media to get their messages out. Follow them. And, they will surely follow you back. Repost their messages. You will garner goodwill by helping in their communications efforts and you may find that you get reposted as well. We have found, in particular, that bar organizations will repost interesting commentary by their members.

Also consider reposting your clients' posts. Be careful, of course, to consult with them before posting. For example, if you are a criminal lawyer, a client might not want people to know they even know you. But there are circumstances where this is a good strategy. If you do a lot of work for startup companies, for example, when those companies have positive news to report, they will appreciate you posting about them. Again, whenever you have communications that involve clients, make sure you are cognizant of ethics responsibilities.

4. *Use social media to communicate with journalists*

One of our surprises with social media is just how easy it is to communicate with reporters and publishers. Many journalists will have conversations with people via social media, and if you are someone who has interesting things to say about the subject they cover, do not be surprised to get a quick response (and a subsequent "follow"). Twitter is particularly good for this. Reporters will often post a story they wrote and then engage in conversation with readers.

Once you build social media relationships with reporters, you will find that you have an easy way to communicate story tips. And reporters may contact you to ask follow-up questions about your posts. There is still a place for old-fashioned press releases, but the odds of getting a reporter's attention are improved if they follow you on social media and you can send them a direct message.

5. *Use social media to amplify your other content*

If you spend a lot of time writing articles, blog posts, newsletters, etc., then you certainly want to maximize the exposure of your writing. You have no doubt seen the social media "share" buttons adjacent to articles you see on the web. Your own blog posts and online articles have those buttons—remember to move them into your various social media accounts. This takes almost no effort and is a great way to get people to read your longer form writing.

Co-author Greg Siskind's blog at blog.ilw.com/gregsiskind has a social media bar at the bottom of each post to allow posts to be shared on

The author's blog at blog.ilw.com/gregsiskind

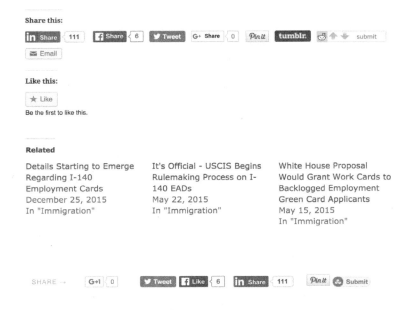

95 Responses to *Siskind Summary: The I-140/AC-21/EAD Proposed Regulation*

various social networks and e-mailed to others. You can post a link on your various social networks by clicking the buttons.

6. *Use social media to have some fun*

Some of the best people to follow on social media are those who post serious, informative content, but who also post about things that have nothing to do with their day jobs. Every now and then, post about things you find interesting that have nothing to do with the law. People like to know you are not all business all the time. It is not unlike a cocktail party where you chat about your out-of-office interests. These days, people are less afraid to delve into "taboo" topics. It used to be a complete no-no to talk to strangers about your views on politics, religion, and sex, for example, or to use foul language. Today, it seems like nothing's off limits. But be careful about over-sharing and filter what you say. Or reserve certain social media as a place where you are not trying to develop business. For example, many people use their personal Facebook pages *only* for their personal lives, and they are not letting people in who are not their friends or family members. If you need to rant about something, post it there, rather than on LinkedIn where you are trying to maintain a consistently professional image.

12

E-mail Marketing

THE BIG PICTURE

Two decades ago, when the first edition of this book was written, e-mail marketing was a critical tool for the first early-adopter lawyers using the Internet to promote their practices. E-mail marketing is still playing a critical role. The big difference today is virtually every client and potential client has an e-mail account and, for many, it is their preferred form of communication. In the old days, you had to send a plain text, impersonalized e-mail to an entire group. Today, there are excellent tools that allow messages to be as good looking as a web page and customized for each recipient. User information can be kept in a sophisticated database and messages can be sent to specific groups of people based on how they are classified in your database.

HOW E-MAIL FITS INTO YOUR CONTENT STRATEGY

E-mail content strategies have not actually changed that much in 20 years. A fundamental initial consideration before determining what will be sent via e-mail is: who *exactly* is the target of the marketing? There are many audiences that may be considered, including:

- Existing clients (who happen to be the source of most referrals)
- Potential clients

- Fellow lawyers from whom you are seeking referrals
- Reporters who are seeking ideas for stories, or who are simply looking to stay educated in the fields they are covering
- Law students

Determining your subject matter requires a similar analysis as you would complete for other online tools, including websites, blogs, and other social media.

- Should you focus on broad topics or niche subjects?
- Should a multi-practice firm produce multipurpose e-mails that cover their various specialties, or should they create separate alerts for each practice area (or, does it make sense to do both)?
- And even within a particular specialty, such as immigration law, should you write to emphasize expertise on even narrower subjects such as international adoptions or sports and entertainment immigration, or cover the range of types of immigration subjects the firm can handle?

Emphasizing a subject that the firm is very interested in promoting is obviously a good way to communicate that you have an exceptional expertise in that area, but there is also a potential sacrifice in ignoring "bread and butter" practice areas. Analyze your competition for "mind-share"—who else is writing about the same topic? What is their angle? How can you be different?

The type of content that can be delivered by e-mail also varies significantly beyond just the substantive areas of law that is the subject of the writing. Examples of what law firms are sending via e-mail include the following:

Newsletters

Newsletters are a great way to deliver a mix of content—analytical articles, updates on the latest news, announcements about firm accolades, introductions to new lawyers and staff, etc. Decide on a frequency that is realistic and stick to it. If you are producing a "monthly" newsletter, make sure it goes out monthly.

Client Alerts/Breaking News

For many years, marketing-smart lawyers have been sending out e-mail alerts to clients summarizing important developments tied to legislation, regulations, case law, and more. Recently, the term "newsjacking" has been coined to describe this phenomenon. Clients and prospective clients benefit from getting valuable information quickly and will recognize that you are relevant and current.

White Papers/Legal Summaries

E-mails are a useful way to deliver a link to a white paper, which includes an in-depth discussion of a particular topic. Greg Siskind has produced "Siskind

Summaries" over the years, providing section by section overviews of major immigration bills. Writing, producing, and distributing those summaries within 24 hours of a bill's passage has become his signature, and the summaries have logged thousands of views in the days after they are released.

Special Occasions (Birthdays, Holiday Cards, and More)

Not every e-mail needs to be substantive and serious. Show your clients you care about them as people—send e-mails to clients and contacts on their birthdays, or on work or wedding anniversaries.

Holiday greeting e-mails have become immensely popular with firms—and some are spending big bucks on these festive communiqués. A lot of these cards are technically websites with the e-mail containing a link to an online card. You do not have to have a large budget to show your clients, prospects, referrals, and friends that you are wishing them well. Be sensitive about religious beliefs when choosing the theme for your holiday greeting.

Announcements of Firm News

E-mail is an easy way to communicate comings and goings at a firm (congratulate a retiring partner, welcome new associates), tout awards and honors, highlight charitable and community leadership positions, link to articles where lawyers are quoted by the media, etc.

Press Releases

In a similar spirit to client alerts, lawyers can publicize their expertise on new legal developments in the form of e-mail press releases. Follow the reporters who cover legal news in your market. Most media outlets include their e-mail addresses in their bylines or on the news outlet's website. They do so because they are inviting the public to send them information, such as tips and news releases.

Links to Video and Audio Content

E-mails can have audio and video content embedded or linked in them. In Chapter 13, we discuss audio and video at greater length, but one way to expand the audience for this content is to use e-mail to push it to a wider audience.

Tying E-mail to Social Media Channels

Content produced in social media, especially popular blog, Twitter, LinkedIn, and Facebook posts, can be delivered via e-mail rather than depending on people finding the content on the web or elsewhere. Likewise, you can invite readers of your blogs to send an e-mail notification to others linking to your post.

Daniel Schwartz's Connecticut Employment Law Blog has a feature allowing readers to e-mail blog posts to themselves or others.

The e-mail feature on Daniel Schwartz's Connecticut Employment Law Blog

Invitations

E-mailing e-vites for firm events, whether they are in person or online events, is smart, given how easy the process has become and how inexpensive it is. You may choose to completely eschew mailing print invitations or publishing print advertisements.

E-MAIL COMPOSITION AND FORMATTING

E-mail, of course, can be quite informal, and that is fine when the situation lends itself to that. But marketing communications sent via e-mail should be treated differently. For starters, sending out messages one at a time or to large lists in your regular e-mail software is not particularly practical. And posting every subscriber's e-mail address in the cc line is unprofessional and impersonal. Using the BCC line and not having the e-mail recipient's e-mail address listed in the "To" field is likely to get your message flagged as spam.

Instead, consider using one of the very good e-mail marketing software programs available (and listed below). The better software programs have a number of key features and advantages over using your own e-mail server including:

- The ability to divide up your e-mail list into subgroups (such as members of particular associations, people in certain occupations, existing clients, prospects, referral sources, people in particular industries, etc.).

- Creation of forms on your website that allow people to subscribe to your publications that are then sent via the e-mail service.
- The ability to customize mass e-mails and embed fields that pull from your database so that each e-mail is individualized as a mail merge. This means the message comes from you and the recipient's own e-mail address is listed in the "To" field, thus reducing the likelihood of being blocked by a spam filter. The recipient's name can also be included in the message (e.g. "Dear John:").
- The ability to design templates (or use templates provided by the software company), which will make the e-mail more attractive and professional. You can design a template that matches your firm's letterhead or make an e-mail that looks similar to a good looking web page.
- Automation of unsubscribe requests so individuals not wishing to receive your mail can easily get off your list. This also makes it easier to comply with federal laws on spamming. (See the ethics discussion in Chapter 17.) Custom autoresponders that send specific e-mails to people requesting information (such as filling out a form to be sent a memorandum you have prepared about a particular subject or sending out a birthday greeting on a subscriber's birthday if they have provided that information previously).
- Relief on your server of the heavy burden of sending e-mail to a large list of subscribers (and possibly exceeding your Internet provider's bandwidth limits).
- Analytics pages that allow you to track key information on the success of your e-mail marketing efforts. Data that can be tracked include the number of people that open your messages versus those ignoring or deleting the message, the number of people that clicked on each web link in your message (something that will help you determine what content people want to read and also how many people visited your website as a result of reading your e-mail), the number of your messages that bounced, and the number of people unsubscribing (important to understanding if you are sending content that is not compelling or you are sending messages too frequently).
- Integration with programs like Google Analytics to help analyze whether your web traffic picked up after an e-mail campaign.

PROVIDERS AND PLATFORMS

There are a number of players in the e-mail marketing software space, so lawyers will have dozens of alternatives. Some of the best known providers are the following:

- MailChimp (www.mailchimp.com)
- Constant Contact (www.constantcontact.com)
- Emma (www.myemma.com)

- Mad Mimi (www.madmimi.com)
- Campaign Monitor (www.campaignmonitor.com)
- Vertical Response (www.verticalresponse.com)
- AWeber (www.aweber.com)
- Topica (www.topica.com)
- Campaigner (www.campaigner.com)

Constant Contact, MailChimp, and Emma are the most popular of the software products. A small to mid-sized firm should expect to pay $50 or so a month for products like these.

Several customer relationship management software systems like InfusionSoft, Salesforce, and Zoho have e-mail management functionality that can offer some of the same features as the e-mail marketing systems listed above.

Another option is to outsource your e-mail marketing to the advertising, public relations, or marketing professional services firm you are already using. Or find a new firm specializing in working with professional services firms on e-mail campaigns.

THE DESIGN OF E-MAILS

Every e-mail—whether it is delivering a newsletter or just a quick update to a client on the status of a case—is effectively a marketing communication since it sends a message about your firm. Aside from the obvious—for example, use correct spelling and grammar—there are a few ways to make your e-mails more effective.

One basic rule is after you have designed your e-mail template (or adapted the template design provided by your e-mail service provider), make sure you test it out on different types of screens and e-mail programs. Remember, people will be reading the e-mail on smartphones, in web browsers on large computers, in dedicated e-mail programs like Outlook, and on tablets. Some may even be reading your e-mail on their watches. Make sure you are comfortable with how your e-mail message looks on those different devices and in different sizes (note, though, that e-mails more than just a few lines in length are generally not viewed on a watch, so you probably do not need to worry too much about that audience just yet).

Also remember that some e-mail programs will render your hypertext markup language (HTML) messages in different ways and some may cut off messages below a certain line and strip out images (or give the recipient the option to turn on images for an individual message). Some of the better e-mail service providers will actually show you how your message will look in the most popular formats before you send your message.

Make sure you choose a subject line for your message that will increase the likelihood that your e-mail will be read. That means not trying to be too clever by choosing a subject line that might make the recipient unsure what the message is covering. They are more likely to hit the delete button than try and guess. Also, focus on how your message will benefit the reader. For example, your subject line might read "5 Ways the New XYZ Regulation Will Affect Your Business."

In earlier editions of this book, we discussed sending e-mails in a text-based or HTML format. HTML e-mails can be viewed like web pages with graphics and links embedded in the message. That discussion is a lot less relevant today as most people view their e-mails using software that can handle HTML. Nevertheless, some programs will strip out images and other coding and just show the reader the text of your message. Some will give the reader the option to click a button and turn all the graphics back on. The takeaway is that you can design your e-mails using HTML so that they look great in most e-mail programs, but you should make sure that your text is not embedded in your graphics so that the message still is readable for people only interested in seeing text.

Signature Blocks

Finally, it is worth spending time talking about signature blocks whether we are talking about a mass mail or a one-off e-mail message. Signature blocks usually are not given much thought. But they have the potential to be either a powerful, free, and easy way to deliver a positive message about your brand and firm to the reader—as important as your business card—or they can just bore or even annoy.

Some people do not have a signature block at all and just sign their name on the end of a message (if that). This might irritate the reader as much as the most overboard signature block. At a minimum, people are often looking for basic contact information about the person writing the message. If you also have not configured your "From" header to list your name, the person receiving the e-mail might not even know who is sending it. If a message is forwarded to you, the lack of a signature block is even more irritating. There is also a pretty good chance you found that message without a signature block in your spam filter even if it was a real message.

At a minimum, a signature block should contain the name, title, phone number, e-mail address, firm name, and website of the author. You can include more information such as your street address, fax number, and other contact details, but most of the time, people are just looking for the basics. The goal should be to limit your signature block to just 3–5 lines of text. If you link to your website, the reader will be able to get more detailed contact information anyway. But providing a phone number and e-mail address is convenient for readers if they do not have the time or inclination to go to your web page. And if they are reading the message on their smartphones, they can just click your signature block's phone number and it will automatically dial you. Also, if you can limit the number of characters on a line, you will avoid words wrapping awkwardly and appearing messy. Try to limit yourself to 72 characters per line.

Beyond the basic contact details, lawyers frequently publish links to social media accounts—Twitter, Facebook, LinkedIn, etc. That is fine, but make sure that if you are linking to these sites, you are regularly posting on them and not writing things that are highly personal or inappropriate for the wide array of potential viewers who will read your e-mails and visit those pages. If you do decide to post links to social media, consider small icons that do not take up a lot of space or just adding text links.

Speaking of images, use graphics sparingly in an e-mail. As noted above, some people still only receive e-mails in a text format, so test what your signature will look like if the recipient does not use an HTML mail program. A small graphic with a firm logo or your signature can look good if it is done tastefully. But if your entire signature block is a graphic image, it can show up in the recipient's mailbox as an attachment.

It is fairly common to see lawyers include extensive disclaimer language in their e-mails. The rule of thumb here is to stick to what your jurisdiction requires, if any, in an e-mail. I would avoid the temptation to throw in the kitchen sink and just include what is necessary. While prudence is never a bad thing, you can go overboard with disclaimers that dwarf the actual e-mail message. There is a healthy debate in the legal community about the effectiveness of e-mail disclaimers. More information can be found in Chapter 17 of this book.

A lot of people include firm tag lines. If you include one, keep it short. Some e-mails include personal sayings that the writer thinks are clever or profound. Usually they are not and we recommend you do not include anything but a short tag line. Sometimes an e-mail is appended with a message like "Sent from my iPhone (or iPad)." This might be helpful to the recipient, because it lets the person know that the sender was e-mailing from a device where they were on the go and could not easily type a lot of text. Ensure that you create a normal signature block as the default on your phones, tablets, and in your regular e-mail program.

Avoid political messages in your signature blocks. Even the "please don't print this message and you'll help save the earth" kind of message will inevitably offend the wrong client. Also, it makes it seem like the sender thinks the reader is an idiot.

And few really care that you won an award or were named to this or that list of lawyers. Again, listing these things leads to signature block bloat. Your signature block is not your resume—do not let your ego coerce you into adding your "Best Lawyer," etc., badges to your block.

Some firms put reminders about major impending changes in the law or other urgent matters that affect a high percentage of the people with whom the lawyer regularly communicates. That can be helpful and worth breaking the usual rules on signature block brevity.

Before you settle on your e-mail signature block, test how it looks in an HTML reader, a plain text reader, and a Rich Text Format (RTF) reader, as well as on phones and tablets. See how your signature block looks if your message is forwarded, particularly if the lines in the message wrapped correctly. Look at your signature block in Outlook, Gmail, and other e-mail clients to make sure there is consistency.

Finally, most of the major e-mail programs allow senders to choose from multiple versions of their signature block and you can pick the one that is most appropriate for the recipient.

DEVELOPING A MAILING LIST

After you have selected an e-mail marketing software system, it is time to build up your mailing lists. But first, a note of caution: Federal rules on spamming are strict, and if an individual complains to your Internet provider, you could find yourself kicked off their service, and server administrators may put you on a black list to block your messages.

There are several places to collect contacts for inclusion. One of the first and easiest places to start is your existing client list. Hopefully, you have a case management system that allows for a list to be easily exported and then imported in to your chosen e-mail system. You will also want to mine your contacts software, whether it is in Outlook, Gmail, or the various other programs people use. Another note of caution: Just because someone is in your contacts database does not mean that you can send e-mail without permission. Send an initial request asking if they are interested in receiving information from you and providing a link to opt in. You can collect information on your website via subscription forms. You can post links to your subscription page in your social media posts. And you can have people sign up the old fashioned way by having subscription forms at your reception desk, at trade shows where you are exhibiting, at events where you are speaking, etc. But when you are collecting cards at an event, such as having a fish bowl in your booth at a trade show, make sure you tell people you are also asking permission to be on your e-mail list.

Finally, do not send e-mail to a purchased list. This will likely violate spam rules and, if the recipient has not given you permission to send them mail, you are also likely violating your state bar's solicitation rules.

Video, Podcasts, and Webinars

13

THE BIG PICTURE

Here are a few compelling statistics that should turn your head:

- According to Cisco, by 2018, video traffic will make up 79 percent of all consumer Internet traffic.
- More than 6 billion hours of video are watched each month on YouTube—that is almost an hour for every person on Earth.
- There are more than 100 hours of video uploaded to YouTube every minute.
- Seventy-six percent of business-to-business (B2B) marketers use video content marketing, states Brightcove, via ReelSEO.
- According to a Gartner research study that is now quite old (2010–2011), video was more than 50 times more likely to appear on the first page of Google, the most important place to drive traffic to your website. There is not a new study to substantiate our belief that this is even more important—and competitive—today.

Video is pervasive and it is consumed, nay devoured, when it shows content about which people care. And this does not mean cat videos and recipe video blogs. People around the world are proving video has captured their valuable attention; consider whether there is a place for your lawyers in this sea of sound and motion. Can you be found without it? Maybe, but firms and lawyers should have strategic conversations about how it fits into their business profiles and plans.

According to Adam Stock, who led law firm Allen Matkins's (www.allenmatkins
.com) video strategy starting in 2010–2011 by converting traditional printed content updates (such as e-alerts) into video, website traffic immediately increased by
15–20 percent. When the firm launched its new video-centric website nine months
later, traffic increased by an additional 30 percent. He says, "Allen Matkins created
video versions of typical law firm communications: alerts, press releases, event
summaries, etc. This approach allowed us to compare the incremental impact of
video to text-only versions." This is described in a presentation/video the firm
produced, which is a helpful primer on how to get started (https://prezi.com
/xsh7ceqplstk/video-for-law-firms-adam-stock/).

A still from https://prezi.com/xsh7ceqplstk/video-for-law-firms -adam-stock/

Allen Matkins started with eight short videos, really as a marketing experiment. Because of its promising results, it turned into a major firmwide effort when
it showed that video was one of the most effective forms of online communication.
In mid-2015, the firm website featured more than 250 videos.

Do videos drive interested visitors to become clients? Stock says, "While it is
hard to track conversion rates, we know anecdotally that attorneys who are in the
videos often meet people who recognize them from their videos. The videos play
a small role in a potential client getting comfortable having one of our attorneys
represent them."

American Bar Association (ABA) *Law Practice* magazine published an article
by Adam Stock called "How Law Firms Are Using Video." Here is a helpful excerpt
from this article:

Brand the practitioner, not the firm

One of the most formidable challenges in legal services marketing is differentiating
legal services. For example, "Law Firm A" has as good of a reputation as "Law Firm

B." For this reason, clients will often say that they "hire the lawyer and not the law firm." If this is true, presenting attorneys in the best light possible should be a primary goal of legal services marketing. By capturing attorneys in action, video places the attorney brand before the firm brand.

For years I hired (and fired) attorneys from highly reputable law firms because the services they provided bore only a loose correlation to the reputation of their firms. The level of service I received was as varied as the attorneys delivering those services. As long as firms market their standings, wins, reputation and expertise rather than the ways their individual attorneys approach problems and deliver service, they are missing a critical element in the legal marketing equation.

Benefits of online video

Online video has shown to have many advantages over other media. It highlights the attorney and provides an opportunity to demonstrate his or her persuasive powers. Through the combination of visuals and sound, video delivers ideas and positions with more authority and emotional impact.

Also, complex information can be explained simply. In fact, because effective videos are two to five minutes in length, they force attorneys to explain issues in a simple format that is ultimately more appealing to prospective clients. Finally, distribution is nearly free. Not only are there no incremental costs for distributing video online—you can post it on YouTube for free—but the medium is in such high demand that others will recommend and share it, thereby assisting in its distribution if the quality is there.

HOW VIDEO AND AUDIO FIT INTO YOUR CONTENT STRATEGY

Do not think of video or audio in a vacuum. Consider it as one highly effective means of distributing valuable content about your important strengths and signature areas. Stock suggests this for video—which also applies to podcasts:

> Explore video versions of every type of communication that you would provide clients and prospects. This approach provides not only a purpose for each video, but a way of evaluating its effectiveness and identifying benefit.

> Each of our videos represents a video version of a regular type of firm communication. This approach allows us to understand the video format's effectiveness in achieving our marketing results. The areas include legal alerts, press releases, educational videos and community involvement videos.

Stock advises any firm interested in pursuing a video strategy, "Don't forget that you are developing online video and not feature films. That should guide a firm's view toward content, length, cost per video, number of videos and distribution."

CHOOSING YOUR SUBJECT MATTER FOR VIDEO AND AUDIO—AND RULES TO LIVE BY

Follow the lesson of Allen Matkins, which focused first on highly technical areas that were important—and perhaps unique—to their firm *and* that were important to target prospects and clients. Choose subject matter that distinguishes your lawyers and about which they can passionately and authoritatively speak.

Avoid videos that smack of lawyer self-promotion. Rather, focus on educating and informing your audience about trends, concerns, horizon issues—things that truly matter to the future of your clients and your law practice.

Adam Stock shares these rules to ensure success:

1. *Publish frequently.* Volume matters in gaining followers and viewers. We publish approximately one new video per week, making them available to clients who access our videos through a subscription.
2. *Keep videos short.* Like blog entries, shorter is better. Based on our experience, online video is best at two to three minutes. We may go up to five minutes for a very technical topic.
3. *Tag and share.* Like blog entries, tag content and share it through social networks and use syndicators to push out content, such as JD Supra and Lexology.
4. *Account for a short shelf life.* Videos have a limited shelf life, so don't make one that will take too long to produce, otherwise the information will be outdated by the time you release it.
5. *Integrate.* Integrate online video into your other forms of marketing. For example, you may find that marketing both through email and video may yield a better result than each of these media alone.
6. *Measure results.* Like all online media, you can measure views, referrals and the number of times videos are shared. Monitor this information via your website analytics tools and learn what works for you.

A CASE STUDY: LAWYER RICHARD HSU

Book author Deborah McMurray is also the author of the Law Firm 4.0 Blog (www .lawfirm4-0blog.com), which has featured several posts about Richard Hsu, a Shearman & Sterling technology partner in Silicon Valley, who has been a standout blogger and podcaster. He developed a video strategy that he featured on his excellent and quirky "One Page Blog" (www.hsutube.com), which is consistent with his to-the-point, no extraneous words approach to communicating. More lawyers should adopt his commitment to concision—clients appreciate it and want it. (The most compelling reason for jumping on the brevity bandwagon—they want it, thus it gets consumed.)

But back to Hsu's video strategy. After viewing several of his videos, McMurray interviewed him to learn more about his strategy and how he did it. Before you watch these (groaning perhaps, thinking they might be typical talking head style continuing legal education videos), understand that no video is longer than 100 seconds and they explain no more than one concept—and that concept had to be conducive to drawing. Wait—drawing, you ask? Watch them at www.hsutube .com and you will see.

Examples of Richard Hsu's videos

Hsu's inspiration was Salman Khan's TED talk about using video to transform education curricula—use simple drawings to illustrate complex concepts. Hsu cannot draw, but his then-13-year old daughter, Maya, could. They used Beyond Pix (http://beyondpix.com) to create the videos, creating six in one highly efficient eight-hour day. To keep cost down, Hsu and Maya created all the content.

Hsu said the response from viewers was and continues to be very positive, and he is getting additional exposure and traffic on one of the kingpin content aggregators, JD Supra (http://www.jdsupra.com/search/searchResults.aspx?sTerm =richard+hsu&x=-1445&y=-10).

Hsu is a left-brain lawyer with a right-brain approach to communicating. It continues to be one of the most unique, appealing, and cost-effective lawyer video strategies.

Richard Hsu and his daughter Maya

Hsu Untied

What you will also see on Hsu Tube is Richard's latest offering, "Hsu Untied," a series of podcast interviews he conducts with lawyers about their burning passions and hobbies outside the office. If you have some time on your hands, listen to the more than 100 episodes—each podcast is 10–16+ minutes long.

Richard Hsu's podcast, Hsu Untied

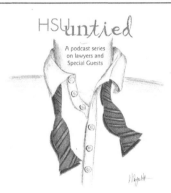

Podcasts have included:

1. *Drew Shoals*, the drummer for the Grammy Award winning band Train. Drew had previously played with the lead singer of Train, Pat Monahan, prior to going to law school. Despite having a successful legal career at Shearman & Sterling, when he got the call to join the band, he could not say no.

   https://soundcloud.com/hsu-untied/dshoals

2. *Wayne Brown*, deputy general counsel and chief intellectual property officer at Quest Diagnostics, who is a tournament chess player. Wayne has a chess rating of "Expert" (top 5–10 percent of all tournament players) and has played competitive chess his entire life—in fact, he cannot remember

a time when he did not know how to move the chess pieces. Wayne discusses his lifelong passion for chess, including his favorite chess openings and how he started beating his dad when he was just in the seventh grade!

https://soundcloud.com/hsu-untied/wbrown

3. *Liz Stone*, a former litigator and now legal recruiter with the Dubin Group, who is also a standup comedienne. Liz actually started doing "stand-up" after a couple of friends noticed her performing a wedding speech and after doing many "open mics," she now performs at clubs like the San Francisco Punchline and Cobbs Comedy Club. Although she enjoys what she currently does, she admits there is nothing more exhilarating—or terrifying—than trying to make an audience laugh.

https://soundcloud.com/hsu-untied/lstone

Richard shows us that successful lawyers are often well-rounded and interesting—and that they have a lot to talk about that does not relate specifically to the practice of law.

Let us get more of them talking.

Making This Considerable Investment and Having It Pay Off

Richard responded to questions that are commonly asked by curious lawyers considering a video or podcast strategy:

1. **How did you get started? How did you know the video blog and podcast series would be a good fit for you and your practice?**

    RH: I started Hsu Tube a few years ago where I developed the legal video series (which ultimately won several awards and received a lot of recognition) with my then-13 year old daughter—mainly because I wanted to learn more about current technology. As my wife said to me at the time I made those videos, "Your problem is that your daughter can't be 13 forever." And indeed, my daughter, who is now 16, has decided to retire.

    Having done video already, I wanted to experiment with the audio medium. Since my childhood dream was to be like Terry Gross (the host and co-executive producer of National Public Radio's Fresh Air), I started by interviewing some lawyer friends with interesting side hobbies. When I started the podcast, I thought I would be lucky if I could find ten people to interview and I am now over 100.

2. **What kind of time commitment do these require?**

    RH: The videos were time consuming. It took an 8-hour day of shooting to make six 2–3 minute videos, excluding all the time to write and develop the content and do all the editing. The podcasts are a *lot* simpler, which is also one of the reasons I decided to switch from video to audio.

3. **How have these investments helped your career and practice? What are the top benefits you have realized from your commitment?**

RH: Let's just say that if I were doing the videos and podcast for the purpose of generating business, I would have stopped a long time ago. Having said that, I have made a lot of new and terrific connections through the process. What has been the most satisfying is how much my guests enjoy the interviews. My favorite reaction was from Santa Clara Law Professor Eric Goldman who said:

A tweet from Eric Goldman about his interview with Richard Hsu

Eric Goldman
@ericgoldman   Follow

Of the hundreds of interviews I've done, this may be my favorite
j.mp/1uzAOOS I talk with @HsuTubeEsq about my slinky
collection
10:17 AM - 9 Aug 2014
2   4

4. **If you had one "do-over," what would you do differently?**

RH: Like a lot of things in life, if I knew how complicated this would have been, I might not have even started. Part of the reason why I think people experiment with new things is because they don't really know what they're getting into!

Richard Hsu had the courage to stand out from the pack, and he is now well known in legal and social media circles because of it. His passion to do something different paid off from a reputation building standpoint—and his circle of business contacts is now at least national, if not extending beyond U.S. borders.

The beauty of the Internet is that the videos and podcasts live on long after the original investment. They are syndicated and shared by others, and until the laws change, his video series will continue to educate potential clients in relevant and engaging ways.

Paul Bonner, director of marketing at Venable LLP, sums up the use of these tools as follows: "The skillful and strategic use of video is a critical element in a comprehensive content marketing strategy. Having one's content 'come to life' builds a more substantive connection with many prospects than the simple written word, and can accelerate the business development process."

GETTING THE RIGHT KIND OF ATTENTION

Given that there are millions of videos on YouTube, how can your video about the marijuana laws in Colorado (well, that actually might get attention on YouTube—bad example)—say the latest regulatory development related to underground storage tanks—how can you expect it to compete for attention? Each video should have its own marketing and distribution plan—remember the audience will be narrow; focus on those people who actually care about your subject matter. Ignore the rest of the world for now.

Here are a few tips that will boost the search engine optimization (SEO) of your video, meaning, it will be easier to find:

1. *Write a descriptive title and a very long video description.* Think of this as a "long-tail" for your video. Include a descriptive title, plus a long description filled with important keywords that are included in the video. The more YouTube knows about your video, the more confidently it can rank it for your target keyword(s). And, more importantly, YouTube uses keywords in the description to rank you for long-tail keywords.

2. *Post your videos on Twitter, LinkedIn, Quora, or Facebook (think of it as self-syndicating).* Your social media followers do not want to see a bunch of lawyer promotional "it's about me" videos, but they do want helpful, authoritative content about what is going on in their fields. Focus on late-breaking issues and areas of law about which they need to know. We have not mentioned Quora before—it is a useful question and answer (Q&A) website, where the Q&A are handled by users—it is all user-generated content.

A page from Quora

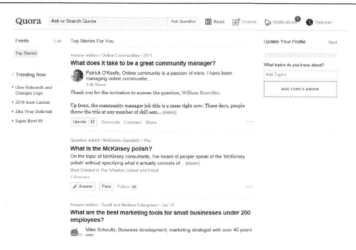

3. *Publish them, of course, to your website.* They should appear on lawyer bios, your home page (if the design accommodates it), relevant practice and industry pages, and news/events pages. It actually will not appear all those places, rather, links to it will appear—but it will launch as though it actually lives on each particular page.

4. *Encourage subscribing and linking to your videos by your viewers.* YouTube pays attention to how popular your video is. Do not be shy about inviting your clients and prospects to like it. This can matter in how YouTube ranks it. Greenberg Traurig has 77 subscribers at the time of this writing—we are

certain the marketing team is focused on boosting this number higher. What is a good number? Any number of people actively following you is good!

Greenburg Traurig's YouTube page

5. *Create a channel for your law firm.* This substantiates your firm and the visitor experience on YouTube. Here is a YouTube link that provides an easy tutorial about how to set up a channel. It is updated regularly, so the link should work, even years after this book was published: https://www.youtube.com/watch?v=N7il-pFZ_Gw.

6. *Once you have 10 or more videos, create a keyword-rich playlist.* Do not leave your YouTube channel a disorganized mess. One of the easiest ways to get more YouTube search traffic to your videos is to organize them into playlists. A keyword-rich playlist gives YouTube deeper information about your video's topic, which enables it to deem it more relevant in keyword searches and drive more views to them.

A playlist on YouTube

PODCASTS

Thanks to the success of radio shows such as TED Radio Hour (http://www
.npr.org/podcasts/510298/ted-radio-hour) and Serial (serialpodcast.org), podcasts
are more popular than ever.

Lifehacker.com has an excellent article (http://lifehacker.com/how-to-start
-your-own-podcast-1709798447) on how to get started, which includes the following equipment list to consider:

- *Microphone(s)* —Any microphone will work for recording your podcast,
  but listeners can usually tell the difference between low and high quality microphones. If you're not sure what to look for, our list of the five
  best desktop microphones is a great place to start (I use four analog
  Audio-Technica AT2020s for my own podcast). As you shop around, you'll
  also need to decide whether you want to use a USB or analog (XLR) microphone. USB mics convert analog sound into digital so you can plug a USB
  mic directly into any computer and start recording without much hassle,
  but you could potentially get lower audio quality compared to analog.
  Considering you don't need any extra tools or devices to record with a
  USB mic, they can be a little cheaper in the long run. Analog microphones
  use XLR connectors, which means you need another device to get your
  audio onto your computer, but you can get higher audio quality and can
  use them with other sound equipment (if you had a PA system or wanted
  to play live music, for example). Of course, if you have a gaming headset
  or other basic microphone around, you can easily use that too.
- *Portable XLR Recorder (optional)*—If you plan on using analog microphones for your podcast, you'll need something that captures your analog
  audio and converts it to digital. Portable XLR recorders can capture multiple microphone channels and allow you to do basic sound level adjusting
  and muting on the fly. Audio files automatically get organized and stored
  on a memory card that you can insert into a card reader or slot in your
  computer. These are amazing tools, but they can be expensive. You can
  find them for anywhere between $100 and $500, depending on how many
  channels and options you need (I use a $400 Zoom H6 Handy Recorder
  with four available analog channels).
- *Audio Interface (optional)*—If you want to record directly to your computer with your analog microphones, you'll need an audio interface. These
  devices allow you to plug in one or more analog microphones and will
  convert the analog audio to digital. Most audio interfaces will connect to
  your computer via USB or Firewire. Audio interfaces can cost as little as
  $30 and go as high as $300, depending on what you need. (You can see
  why a USB microphone is a cheaper option.)
- *A Computer*—Any Windows computer or Mac should work fine to record,
  edit, and upload your podcast. Thankfully, editing audio doesn't take a

ton of computing power. Additionally, depending on how you choose to record—directly to the computer or onto a dedicated recording device—your computer will also need the right ports. USB microphones, for example, will obviously need an open USB port. If you're using analog microphones with a portable XLR recorder or audio interface device, you'll need either a 3.5 mm audio-in jack, a USB port, or in some cases, a Firewire port. So before you spend any money on equipment, make sure you have a computer that can support it.

- *Audio Editing Software*—For the actual recording and editing, you'll need a Digital Audio Workstation (or DAW), there are a lot of good options out there, but the licenses for some of them can cost a pretty penny, though. Licenses for professional level DAWs like Reason or Pro Tools can cost anywhere between $300 and $900. Because of that, most people will recommend free open source programs like Audacity when you're just getting started . . .
- *Pop Filters (optional)*—The clearer your audio can sound, the better. Pop filters, while not required, are fairly cheap and can keep your plosives from making a nasty sound on your recording. If you don't want to buy any, though, you can make some of your own (http://linkon.in/nomore pop).

    You might be thinking that all this equipment is pretty expensive, and you are not wrong. However, keep in mind that decent audio equipment will last forever if you take care of it. It may be expensive to get started, but after the initial purchase, you're set.

And, Ruth Carter, popular blogger (read her blog at http://www.undeniableruth .com/) and podcaster, published nine no-nonsense rules for ensuring success as a podcaster. It is not too late to jump onto this bandwagon, but be smart about it. This list was originally posted on the Attorney at Work blog (www.attorneyatwork .com).

1. *Being a podcaster doesn't make you special—creating excellent content does.* Your job as a podcaster is to create quality content. Don't get into podcasting just to say that you have a podcast. If you don't have good content, you won't have listeners.
2. *Ask for help.* It can be intimidating to start a podcast. There are lots people who are willing to help you with things you may not be an expert in like editing and graphic design. You will make yourself insane if you try to do everything on your own.
3. *Your podcast can open doors.* You can leverage your podcast for professional advancement. It could open the door for books, public speaking and jobs. A podcast is an exceptional tool for creating a professional niche.
4. *Have a co-host.* In general, podcasts work better when you have a co-host. You can only talk to yourself so much. It's much more effective and fun

to have someone to banter with. My favorite legal podcast is Blind Drunk Justice, cohosted by two anonymous lawyers known only as BL1Y and The Namby Pamby. Part of what made their podcast so enjoyable was the way they interacted with each other, not just the topics they discussed. Another way to liven up your podcast is to invite guests to be on an episode.

5. *The f-word is overrated.* The [Federal Communications Commission] doesn't regulate podcasts. There are no "deadly words" that you can't say in your show. It's okay to swear on your podcast—I've done it—but don't do it every two seconds. You can say anything you want when you record your show and then edit it before you release it to maximize your impact.

6. *Release a new episode every week.* Ideally you should release new episodes on the same day every week. Your listeners will expect and look forward to it. Your listeners will also appreciate your show having some type of structure so they know what to expect every week.

7. *Your show should cover the topic of the week, and then stop.* Each episode "should be as short as you can possibly make it." Don't add anything just to fill time. Listeners often listen to podcasts when they're working out and in the car. They won't listen to a show if they think it's too long. Many podcast episodes are about 30 minutes long, but they can be shorter. Legal Lad does one tip per show. He rarely has an episode that's more than six minutes long.

8. *Invest in a quality microphone and headphones.* There are ways to save money when making a podcast, but you shouldn't scrimp on these. Your microphone and headphones make a huge difference in your sound quality. Talk to experts to find the right microphone for your voice.

9. *Don't plan to recoup your investment.* Think of your podcast as a hobby. It's something you do for fun because you love it. Never go into a podcast with the intent of making money. That might happen, but it definitely isn't the norm.

Dennis Kennedy and Tom Mighell are the hosts of a popular podcast on law office technology called the Kennedy-Mighell Report. The two hosts recently broadcast an excellent episode entitled "Practical Podcast Tips," which is linked at http://www.tkmreport.com/2016/10/23/kennedy-mighell-report-178-practical-podcasting-tips/.

Podcasting is a terrific medium for lawyers in any size firm—solos, small firms, and global firms all have successful stories to tell. Following Ruth's guidelines, the best place to start is identifying your passions. You will not be consistent or successful unless you love your content—and your energy, enthusiasm, and top quality will prompt your listeners to love it, too.

Richard Hsu has already been highlighted in this book for both his videos and his podcast series, "Hsu Untied." Other successful podcasters include Sam Glover and Aaron Street at Lawyerist.com.

A podcast on Lawyerist.com

Legal Talk Network is a terrific source for podcasts geared exclusively to lawyers.

Podcasts on Legal Talk Network

PRODUCTION OPTIONS AND BEST PRACTICES

In the world of smartphones and a webcam on every laptop computer, it is easy to quickly produce videos. And the quality of the video one can produce with those tools has dramatically improved—as has video recording with your smartphones. So, does a lawyer wanting to add video to a website need professional assistance, or is do-it-yourself the way to go?

It may depend on the context, on your budget, and how natural you are in front of the camera. If you are going to have one video that will, for example, be embedded on the front page of your website or in your social media profiles, you might want to invest several thousand dollars to get the video professionally scripted and produced. Even if you plan to use video regularly, you should consider at least starting with a professional video production firm until you are really familiar and comfortable with the video production process. Later on, when you are no longer a novice, you can consider investing in good equipment and training and film your videos in-house.

You can also spend a little less, but produce a series of videos. The regular updating will help build traffic and get search engine traffic. A great example of a series of short videos posted by a law firm is Baker Donelson's Entrepreneur Minute.

Maybe you are a natural in front of the camera, but a lot of videos on law firm websites are, frankly, cheesy and embarrassing. The best are those showing lawyers talking naturally, they are very brief—maybe 30 seconds to two minutes long—they have good editing, lighting, and sound, and they should be more conversational and not salesy.

Baker Donelson's Entrepreneur Minute

Your introduction video should be scripted. But other types of videos might appear more extemporaneous (this does not mean they are seat-of-the-pants, though). A good outline and serious rehearsing will make you sound polished and authoritative. Looking straight at the camera is best when it is just you speaking— watch that you do not have shifty eyes. Another approach is to have someone off camera (or on) interview you—in this case you would look more at the interviewer and not at the camera.

Depending on the region in which you are getting your videos produced, the cost can range from $4,000–6,500 per finished minute. Production costs are often aggregated and quoted as a "per finished minute" cost. This includes equipment and often includes scripting, make-up, pre- and post-production, and any B-roll segments (supplementary footage designed to enhance the main video) and music that you use.

DISTRIBUTION: YOUTUBE, VIMEO, AND LIVE STREAMING OPTIONS

Once you have produced the videos, what do you do with them? Many choose to embed the videos in the website to boost interactivity and engagement. In addition, to boost views, post them to video sites like YouTube and Vimeo. Everyone is familiar with YouTube—primarily for cat and flash mob videos—and it is the second largest search engine in the world, and gets hundreds of millions of unique views per month. On YouTube, once you have posted a video (unless you set up a "channel" and purchase advertising for your firm), you have essentially given up control. The greatest advantage to YouTube distribution is that it is owned by Google, which makes a video more likely to be picked up in the Google search engine than a video posted elsewhere. If you limit yourself to the free version of YouTube, you may find a competitor has purchased and placed an advertisement on the very page your video is posted.

Setting up a YouTube channel is free. YouTube allows you to accept advertisements and get a cut of the revenue, but most lawyers will want to opt to remove them. You simply need to deselect the radio button next to "Allow advertisements to be displayed alongside my videos" when you manage the video you have uploaded. There are several good resources about this on the Internet. See Attorney at Work's article "Let Video Market Your Legal Services" (https://www.attorneyatwork.com/let-video-market-your-legal-services/) or, for a good example, watch lawyer Gerry Oginski's videos about the subject at his YouTube channel (https://www.youtube.com/user/lawmed1).

Vimeo does not have advertising, has a cleaner layout, and is generally the more "serious" of the two sites. Also, Vimeo, unlike YouTube out of the box, offers a premium service that allows a lot more customization than YouTube, so it has become popular with businesses.

Expand your goals and embed your videos elsewhere—on your blog and on other social media, such as your Facebook page, LinkedIn profile (via SlideShare), Avvo, and Twitter. You will simply take the embed code and paste it into your website or blogging software. You may need to get your site software updated with a plug-in in order to allow for such posting, but that is usually a fairly easy and inexpensive service request.

Both YouTube and Vimeo allow you to create a channel to group all of your videos in a single location. Having a channel is also a way to build a video brand online. You can customize these pages and include your own graphics. On both sites, you can provide a description and add tags so that search engines have an easier time picking up the videos. You can also transcribe your content and add it to the video, which helps in getting picked up in a search engine.

A new social media tool that has gotten a lot of attention recently is live video streaming. Actually, video streaming has been around for years, but not with the same social media aspects that we see today with products like Periscope, Meerkat, and Blab. Facebook can also now be used for live streaming with its Facebook Live tool. Periscope and Facebook Live are particularly enticing because of the easy access that Periscope offers to Twitter's 300 million users and that Facebook Live offers to Facebook's one billion users. Each allows people using their smartphones to stream video out to their followers. Periscope is the market leader largely because it is owned by Twitter, and Twitter users have an easy time channeling their content to the followers they already have on there.

Live streaming may change the way lawyers think about video. Obviously, you are not using professional production techniques and no one expects you to use anything other than your smartphone to be recording video. But it is an easy way to live stream seminars and any other live events where a lawyer is participating (and which can be permissibly televised, i.e., not the courtroom). Though these streaming tools are only a few months old as of this writing, a number of lawyers have already used them in their marketing. You might consider using a tripod made for a smartphone (there are dozens available for purchase on Amazon) or have someone helping to film other than the lawyer. You can also opt to have the video footage archived on your phone. Periscope, for example, can be configured so that this happens automatically.

Entrepreneurial San Diego immigration lawyer Jacob Sapochnick has had success using various live streaming tools, including Facebook and Periscope. His Facebook page at https://www.facebook.com/myimmigrationlawyer/videos has dozens of videos he has created on immigration law and he has live streamed seminars through new social network video tools so people unable to attend in person are able to watch online.

A video by Jacob Sapochnick on Facebook

Search Engine Marketing and Search Engine Optimization (SEM and SEO)

Tim Stanley, Ken Chan, and David Kemp, Justia

THE BIG PICTURE—WHAT IS SEO?

Search engines help people locate information on the Internet by returning a list of web pages that are relevant to a search query. Some of these search results are advertisements, and require a monetary payment from the website owner to the search engine for each click, user action, or impression that the search engine delivers. The remaining results, called organic listings, do not require a payment to the search engine, and are based on how each search engine weighs different quality factors in its algorithm.

Search engine optimization (SEO) focuses on the organic results, and seeks to improve the placement of websites in the organic listings. The ultimate goal is to appear on the first page of the search results because websites on those pages receive the most clicks. Law firms that implement an effective SEO strategy to promote their content-rich websites can attract substantial increases in visitor traffic and inquiries from potential clients.

This chapter focuses on Google, the dominant search engine in the U.S. market, because much of what is true for Google also applies to Bing, Baidu, and the other search engines. Depending on the particular search terms entered, Google may display the organic results at the top of the page, underneath the ads, or below the local results.[1] The organic search results from Google are circled below.

Organic search results on Google

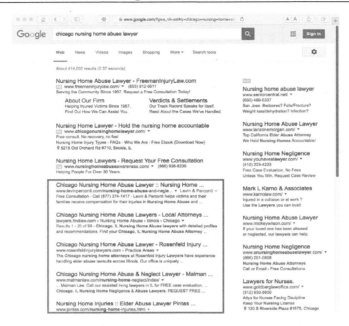

The four core components of SEO are (1) content, (2) markup, (3) structure, and (4) distribution.

1. *Website Content* is the written content of the website that is visible to every visitor. Law firm websites, at a minimum, typically include a home page, attorney biographies, and practice area pages.
2. *Website Markup* is the hidden code that instructs the browser on how to format a web page. It is also used by search engines to identify key characteristics about the website, and includes title tags, meta descriptions, page headings, and schema markup for elements such as the firm's address.
3. *Website Structure* is the organization of the different components of a website. It includes the sitemaps, content hierarchy, and server setup and affects how easily search engines can crawl and index a website for inclusion in search results.

---

1. We are not covering local/map results in this chapter. That said, the same factors that related to SEO for the organic search results also apply to the local results, although there are additional factors for the local results including the actual location of the business and business name, address, and phone number (NAP) consistency in yellow page and online directories.

Particularly for Google, local/map results have undergone many changes in recent years and almost anything in written text will be obsolete very quickly. You can learn more about local/map results at Search Engine Land: http://searchengineland.com/library/channel/local.

4. *Website Distribution* focuses on how other web pages link to the website. This includes external inbound links to the website home and internal pages, along with links, shares, and likes from associated social media profiles.

Before we discuss in greater detail each of the enumerated items above, we want to make one important point. If you get nothing else from this chapter, remember this key to SEO success:

> *Your website must have high-quality, original, focused content.*

SEO is constantly changing, and we cannot cover everything or be totally up-to-date in a printed book. We will cover the core areas, but will also highlight some resources at the end of this chapter where you should be able to get up-to-date information.

But some things are timeless. So let us repeat this one more time here for emphasis, as there is nothing more important to obtaining high ranking in the search engines:

> *Your website must have high-quality, original, focused content.*

With that, let us start with a discussion of website content, and what it means to have high-quality, original, focused content.

WEBSITE CONTENT

The key to SEO success for law firms is writing high-quality, original, focused content. This requires an upfront commitment of time and resources. That said, you should derive real long-term benefits from writing the content, as once it is written, most material does not need to be updated very often. Investing your time and energy in writing high-quality, original, focused content for your website is the most cost-effective strategy for online marketing.

We can divide our discussion of high-quality, original, focused content into its individual components: high-quality content, original content, and focused content. After covering these basics, we will then discuss what to write about.

High Quality Content

Any content you publish on your website needs to be high quality, so that it reflects well on you and your reputation. Search engines also are interested in websites with high-quality content because they want to refer their users to authoritative sources.

Google, in particular, has focused on identifying and providing higher quality content, with its updates to their search ranking algorithm, called Panda, which started in 2011 and has continued since.[2]

Panda seeks to prevent low-quality content from ranking highly in its search results. Currently, Google filters all content in its index on a periodic basis, so if you have low-quality content that is caught in the Panda filter, even if you improve your content, it may take some time before your ranking improves. Google has stated that it plans to filter continuously at some time in the future, so your ranking should improve more quickly when you improve your content.

How is quality measured? Search engines evaluate a number of factors to determine the quality of a web page. Some quantifiable elements of a written page that the search engines can use as proxies for quality include page length, spelling, grammar, and keyword density (which is used to detect text spam). Other factors that may be used to measure quality are harder to understand, such as the uniqueness of words used on the page (e.g., using terms not found on other web pages, such as legal terms, increases the probability that the page will not be penalized by the Panda filter).

Search engines like web pages with substantial content. Having more content is seen as a signal of quality. If you have too few words of content on a particular web page, that page's ranking will tend to be low and will get little, if any, referral traffic from the organic search results.

A search-engine-optimized web page should have at least 500 words of unique content. And while the page might not need 500 words to rank for all search terms, meeting the 500-word threshold will serve you well for all searches on Google at this time.[3]

Some webmasters have seen gains in ranking by writing even more than 500 words. Currently there seems to be some increased rankings for simply writing more content, up to 650 words; that is, you will likely not see an increase in a page's ranking on Google just for writing more words beyond 650 words. That said, you are welcome to write longer pages, and certainly you can rank for additional terms that you might add into the extended text. It is just that your page is not being rewarded simply because it is longer.

It is important to note that word count refers to the unique content on the web page; it does *not* include text that is on every page of the website, such as text in the header, sidebar, or footer. Sometimes there might be an initial jump in rankings for shorter written content on a new or redesigned website, but eventually Google will index all of the pages of the website and distinguish the unique content on

---

2. At the time of this writing, we are currently at Panda 4.2. See Search Engine Land for a more detailed overview and news about Google's Panda updates, *at* http://searchengineland.com/library /google/google-panda-update.

3. This word length of a page for SEO has increased over time; at one point it was 250 words. And we know there are examples of pages ranking for some search terms with fewer than 500 words, but this is not true for all search terms. Our recommendation is to write at least 500 words to protect yourself from any downside.

each page from that which appears site-wide. The website's ranking may suffer if the unique content is not long enough.

For these reasons, writing at least 500 words, and ideally 650 words, of original content on each web page will help your web page perform well in Google search results.

You also need to make sure that content has been checked for spelling and grammar. Open up Microsoft Word or another word processing program and do a spelling and grammar check on the content.

Finally, ensure that your content is useful to the reader. If it is just pieced together sentences and paragraphs, it will not rank well. Google does a very good job at knowing the difference between content that is written to game the SEO system and content that provides real value to the reader, even if there are some SEO features included in the content. Write content that you can be proud of—it will help your web page rank better.

Original Content

Originality is the second key component when search engines approximate quality. Search engines do not want to rank two pages with the exact or substantially similar content highly in their search results. In nearly all cases, the original version of the content will be the one that ranks higher.[4]

You can check the originality of your content by using a service like Copyscape (http://www.copyscape.com), which matches the text of a web page against other web pages. We recommend purchasing the Copyscape paid service, which costs five cents per search.

Do not worry about duplicate content that is from your header, sidebar, or footer of your own website. Google and other search engines will recognize them as part of your site structure and will not hold that against you. Nor should you be concerned if you have a small amount of content that appears elsewhere on the Internet. Your content might include a quote from a state statute or a blog feed; as long as you give the original author attribution, it is not a problem.

However, you need to have at least 500 words of original content in addition to the duplicate content. If you do have duplicate content on your web page (not including the header, sidebar, or footer of the website itself), try to have a 2:1 ratio of original content to duplicate content. For example, if you have a 300-word quote, try to have 600 words of original content (for a total of 900 words on that page). In

---

4. There are exceptions to this rule, such as when the duplicate content is on a domain that Google highly trusts, especially if the duplicate content is placed on this trusted domain very shortly after it initially goes up. For lawyers this tends to be an issue with blog posts or articles showing up on certain article distribution websites, such as JD Supra (http://www.jdsupra.com). If you do wish to distribute your articles and blogs to third party websites, ask the website to add your content at least one month after you initially post it, so that Google gives your blog the original author credit and ranks your content above the distribution website. JD Supra in particular has been able to do this with blogs for our clients, giving them an additional distribution channel without interfering with their organic SEO.

addition, try to put the original content before the duplicate content on the page. Content that appears higher on a page tends to be given more weight than that which appears further down.

If you have multiple pages on your website that have substantial similar content to each other—enough to be considered duplicative—you can address the issue either by rewriting one of the pages, or by using a canonical tag for one of the pages so that Google knows both pages are substantially the same and that Google should only rank one of them.[5]

Finally, if someone has copied your content, check to see whether you are ranking higher for it. Copy a sentence or two of the content from your web page and paste it into Google's search field. If your web page with that content ranks higher than the other web page that has it, you are probably fine and the person copying it is likely being punished. If the other web page is ranked higher, then you can either contact the person who copied it and ask them to remove it, file a Digital Millennium Copyright Act (DMCA) request with Google and the other search engines to have them remove the page that copied yours,[6] or rewrite your content.

If you copied someone else's content, then write an original page and replace the copied content, for both ethical and SEO reasons.

Focused Content

In addition to writing high-quality, original content, you need to write about the subjects for which you want to rank. For example, if you want to rank for (and thus reach clients in) Denver, then you should use the word "Denver" on your web page (and for larger cities like Denver, the page itself should be focused on Denver, as opposed to trying to incorporate an entire region of smaller cities).

For competitive terms, it is important to ensure that the web page markup is also focused on the term (e.g., the <title> tags and meta descriptions should be properly used, as discussed in the "Web Page Markup" section, below).

In general, we recommend that you try to use variations of the key terms on the web page, by using synonyms and/or varying the order of the words. Google associates words with their synonyms, such as "lawyer" and "attorney," or "car" and "auto." Going back to our previous example, you might use synonyms and vary the order of the words on your web page, and thus could have: (1) Denver car accident lawyer, (2) auto accident attorney in Denver and (3) Denver lawyer

---

5. A canonical meta tag is an HTML markup element that specifies the preferred version of a web page. We are not going to go into details about canonical tags in this chapter, but you can learn more about them at the following URLs: https://support.google.com/webmasters/answer/139066 and https://moz.com/learn/seo/canonicalization.

6. Google might not remove a web page for editorial reasons, but they are very good at removing copyright violations. Google's DMCA Dashboard is part of their Google Search Counsel (formerly Webmaster Tools) and can be found here: https://www.google.com/webmasters/tools/dmca-dashboard.

Bing also accepts DMCA removal requests at https://www.bing.com/webmaster/tools/contentremoval form/.

handling car accidents. Google will associate these terms as being the same, and it will often make your page easier for human readers to read and understand.

But do not overuse a term. If you overuse a term, Google might punish your page for that particular term alone in the search results. We have seen instances where a lawyer has used the same term on a single page in excess of 40 times. Do not do this; it will definitely not help, and it can potentially be disastrous. Be reasonable in how many times you use a term.

What to Write

Now that you understand what high-quality, original, focused content is, the question remains what pages to write. A law firm website can be broken down into five main categories of pages:

1. Website Home Page
2. About the Firm Page
3. Attorney Profiles
4. Practice Areas
5. Frequently asked questions (FAQs) and Articles

Obviously, law firm websites can feature more pages than this, but these are the essential ones from an SEO standpoint.

Website Home Page

This is the most important page for SEO primarily because it is the page that most third-party websites (such as directories) will link to. (See the "Editorial Links" section below.)

Take extra care to see that your home page text meets all the requirements described above for high-quality, original, focused content. We see many websites that want a "clean" design and do not wish to have much content on the home page. You certainly can do this—it is your website—but do not expect Google to rank your home page very high if you have minimal content on it. A good designer should be able to work with you to make a clean design that still has 500–650 words of content.

The other thing to note is that you cannot focus on every term on your home page. Try to either pick the more competitive terms, like "Denver Personal Injury Lawyer," or if you feel you cannot compete for that term, then choose a secondary term like "Denver Car Accident Lawyer." It is better to be on the first page of Google results for a secondary term than on the second page of results for a more competitive term.

Again, opting for clean design is fine, but we recommend that your home page has at least 500–650 words of high-quality, unique, focused content if you want your page to rank well in Google.

About the Firm

Most law firms have an "About the Firm" page and individual attorney profile pages. Both of these types of pages should get significant traffic because they are often included in the website's global navigation, such as the navigation bar, and will show up in organic search results for firm name and attorney name searches.

The "About the Firm" page can be optimized for a secondary practice area that is not chosen for the home page. For example, if the home page is optimized for "Denver Personal Injury Lawyer," you might want to optimize the "About the Firm" page for "Denver Accident Lawyer." In most cases, we recommend using the location of the law firm's main office as the geographical term to focus on for the "About the Firm" page.

Attorney Profiles

Individual attorney profiles also receive a significant amount of traffic—often more than any other pages of the website. Most of it comes from searches for lawyer names. For individual profiles, we recommend that the primary optimization be for the name of the attorney. This helps lawyers manage their online reputation by controlling what is displayed when someone searches for their names. Secondary optimization for attorney profiles can be the location of the office where the attorneys work, along with their main practice areas, and of course the word "lawyer" or "attorney."

We also recommend that attorneys link to their social media and lawyer directory profiles from their individual profile page on their website, and vice versa (more on this in the "Social Media" section below). It is important to maintain control of your online reputation, and the best way to do that is to optimize for your name with substantial content on your site and other online profiles you control.

Practice Areas

In addition to the lawyer profiles, practice area pages are the core of most law firm websites. Law firms should write individual pages that target all substantive aspects of their practice. For example, a divorce law firm website should have more than a single practice area web page focused solely on divorce. A best practice is to author practice descriptions that target all the topics, which commonly arise in a divorce case, such as divorce, collaborative divorce, property division, alimony, child support, child custody, alimony modification, and pension benefit division. Each page can then be optimized for a different practice area or topic and location (such as a city, county, or state).

Each page you write on a subject can help the previously written pages by showing Google that the subject matter as a whole is being covered in depth on your website. Having many quality pages will increase the practice area domain authority of your website for that practice area, which in turn improves your Google ranking.

FAQs and Articles

FAQs and articles tend to be popular pages on lawyer websites. FAQs generally do slightly better in the search results than generic articles, as many users phrase their queries in the form of a question when they search. We recommend writing one question and answer per page. But if you are unable to write 500 words for a single question and answer, you can combine multiple questions and answers into a single page.

Some lawyers write focused articles about smaller cities and towns near their office in an attempt to get some increased search engine traffic from these areas. This can work well if you have high-quality original content. However, do not use a Mad Libs approach;[7] put in the effort to make each page unique and add in legal content—for example, define the legal process for civil litigation in your city, or legal defenses in a criminal case in your state—not just generic information about the town's history or tourist attractions. Finally, do not copy directly from the Wikipedia page for the city or town.

Additional Items about Content

We would like to address a couple additional items about content: multiple languages and fresh content. Because users of the Internet speak a multitude of languages, it is increasingly important for those using it for marketing to know and reach all of their prospective audiences, regardless of language. Freshness of content is another aspect of content marketing that is especially important for topics likely to be in the news.

Multiple Languages

Lawyers seeking to reach clients in ethnically diverse communities should publish their content in multiple languages. This can help the lawyer attract clients who do not speak English or who do speak English but prefer to communicate in their native tongue. If an attorney, paralegal, or another professional at your law firm (or a translation service your law firm uses) is fluent in another language, you can use that to expand your marketing reach.

If you want to rank well in a language besides English, you need to include website content in that language. One of the benefits of having web pages in languages other than English is that there is less competition in the search engines for rankings. Additionally, you do not need to write new content, but just to translate your existing English content.

---

7. A Mad Libs approach would be having a locality variable that is substituted into a general template for each locality page. Google can easily detect this and will not rank the pages. You can get the Mad Libs app and books at http://www.madlibs.com if you want to learn more about what *not* to do on your website.

Google's high-quality content requirements for non-English content are the same as they are for English content: You should *not* use an automated translation tool to publish translated content on your website. One of the factors that Google uses in determining the quality of content is grammar. Translation tools can be useful for a non-speaker to understand the gist of a page in a foreign language, but entire translated sentences and paragraphs may be rife with grammatical errors.

Moreover, you have a legal website, and you do not want to misstate the law. An automated translation tool might provide a grammatically incorrect translation that also erroneously states your legal analysis. Having many low-quality foreign language pages on your website can negatively affect your site's rankings as a whole, negating any high-quality English pages.

Having your content in other languages can be very useful as long as you devote the effort or resources to ensure that content matches the quality of your English-language pages. Translate your content on your own or hire a professional translator for your website. Do not use automated tools or low-quality translators. This is not the place to try to save a few bucks.

Fresh Content

Google has said that fresh content will rank higher in search rankings,[8] which is why we encourage law firms to continually add content to their websites.

For inspiration, law firms should look to new laws, court decisions, or other legal developments that impact their practice. By analyzing current legal issues, lawyers can update the content on their websites, attract potential clients who are facing similar problems, or even garner media attention as a legal authority figure.

Many law firms do not have the resources to provide weekly updates on the law. That is understandable. However, law firms should keep abreast of the law and periodically review their website to ensure that their content reflects the current state of the law.

If you are not updating the content on the website directly, but you are blogging or participating in social media, then you might include those blog feeds or social media updates into your website to give your website fresher updated content.

WEB PAGE MARKUP

In this section, we will discuss web page markup and primary tags that can affect a web page's SEO. A web page consists of text and HTML (hypertext markup language) or XHTML (extensible hypertext markup language) markup language. The text is typically all you see when a browser, such as Edge, Internet Explorer,

---

8. *See* Google, *Giving You Fresher, More Recent Search Results* (2011), *at* https://googleblog.blogspot.com/2011/11/giving-you-fresher-more-recent-search.html.

Firefox, Safari, or Chrome, interprets the markup. The markup defines the structure and presentation of the text and other objects. For example, to make the text "Law Firm" bold, you would put it within tags Law Firm.

While tags are primarily intended to define the structure or presentation of a page, Google and other search engines have determined that text within certain tags is a good indicator of what is on the page. Thus, the placement of text within specific HTML tags can affect the ranking for the page for the terms within those tags. Some of this markup is visible on the page itself, such as <h1> and <h2> header tags, and actually changes the way the text or other elements on the page appear to the user, while other markup is not visible, such as schema markup for a locality, on the page but still helps Google determine what the page is about. "Schema markup" is code that you put on your website to help the search engines return more informative results for users.

In this section, we discuss the primary tags that can affect a web page's SEO. There are also links to resources on the web for more detailed information about HTML and XHTML markup.

Title Tags

The first and most important tag is the title tag, which should identify what the page is about, much like the tab on a paper file folder. It is what shows up at the top of the browser for any given web page, what is displayed by default when you add a page to your bookmarks, what is shown when you share or like a page in social media, and often what is displayed in the snippets used in the Google search results.

Here is an example title tag for a page about car accidents by Chicago personal injury lawyer Robert Kreisman:

<title>Car Accidents :: Chicago Auto Accident Lawyer Robert Kreisman</title>

The HTML markup <title> and </title> markers tell Google the title of the page. In this case the page is focused on car accidents, so we start the title tags with those words. We want people to know that this is a page written by an injury lawyer in Chicago, and is likely to have information that is focused on car accident law in Chicago, as opposed to a medical site about car accident injuries or a web page focused on Los Angeles laws. Thus we add in the words "Chicago Auto Accident Lawyer" as a descriptive term before the lawyer's name. The lawyer's name is the least important text from an SEO perspective, but we put that at the end to let users know who wrote the page, and for branding purposes if the page is shared on social media.

From an SEO perspective, the title tag is the most important text on the page. However, there are a few caveats. First, the words in the title tag also need to appear in the body of the web page. This may seem obvious, as the title tag is supposed to describe the web page. But, we have seen many law firm web pages with keywords in the title tag that are missing from the web page itself.

Second, Google generally shows up to 60 characters of text in their search results. After 60 characters, Google will replace the end of the title with an ellipsis ("..."). Thus, shortening the title tag to 60 or fewer characters is preferred to have the full title show up in the search results. If limiting the title tag to 60 characters is impractical, move the more important terms to the first 60 characters. You should also know that if the tag does not describe the page, Google might change it in the search results. Google also changes the appearance of its search results based on the user search term. For example, if you search for your firm name, Google will often display just your firm name as the title of your home page instead of the text that actually appears in the title tags.

As title tags are often used in the Google snippets, they can also increase the click-through rate on the Google search results page. Having a higher click-through rate can also increase the web page's ranking in the Google search results. Thus, try to write a title tag that appeals to your target audience.

A search result from Google with a title tag in the first line

Car Accidents :: Chicago Auto Accident Lawyer Robert ...
www.robertkreisman.com/**auto-accidents**.html ▾
Call Now for a Free Consultation at (800) 583-8002. Available 24/7. Robert Kreisman
represents folks in **Auto Accident** and **Car** Collision cases in **Chicago** and ...

Third, many social media websites will use the title tag of a page as the text for a link when someone shares the web page. The words in these links can help a page rank higher for those terms. Thus, having a good title tag can lead to better links.

Finally, each web page should have a unique title tag. Google tends to favor unique title tags for each page because it helps the search engine understand how the pages are different. Unique title tags also help your website from an SEO perspective because Google seldom ranks two pages from the same website for a competitive search term. Thus, two pages with identical title tags will likely be competing with each other, with only one ranking.

Meta Descriptions

Meta description information is contained in the <meta description> tag within an HTML or XHTML page and is generally not visible when a page is rendered. One use of the meta is to provide text that Google and other search engines can use to create the snippets (the short description of each result) on their search results page if one or more of the searched terms appears in the meta description.

<meta name="description" content="Call Now for a Free Consultation at (800) 583-8002. Available 24/7. Robert Kreisman represents folks in Auto Accident and Car Collision cases in Chicago and Cook County."/>

Because meta descriptions show up in the snippets in the search results, if written well, they can increase the probability of clicks from the search results page. Increased clicks to a particular page can increase the ranking of that page in the search results because it is a sign to Google that the destination page contains the information the user was seeking. Thus, while the text in the meta description does not impact the ranking of a web page directly in the same way that title tag text does, it does impact the rankings indirectly by potentially increasing clicks to the page. Again, you can look at the Google search results snippets, which show the meta descriptions for some searches. If you don't add a separate meta description, search engines will pick up the first 140–150 characters of the page. Ensure that you write a rich first sentence with meaningful keywords. Jones Day appears in a search for "internal investigations employment" and Sheppard Mullin appears in a search for "wage and hour class actions."

Google search result snippets from two searches

[PDF] CORPORATE INTERNAL INVESTIGATIONS best ... - Jones Day
www.**jonesday**.com/files/.../CII%20Best%20Practices%20Pitfalls%20to%20Avoid2.pd... ▾
corporate internal investigation protected by the attorney- client privilege can ... issues in **internal investigations**, joint defense agreements, the effective use of ...

Wage and Hour Class Actions: Sheppard, Mullin, Richter & Hampton ...
www.sheppardmullin.com/**wage-and-hour-class-actions** ▾
Defending, managing and resolving **class actions** requires experience and creativity. Sheppard Mullin represents clients in the defense of employment and ...

Like title tags, each page should have its own unique meta description. Google wants you to consider carefully the content of the page you are describing. In general, meta descriptions should be 150 characters or fewer.

There is also a meta keyword tag. Search engines no longer use meta keywords for any purpose. Sometimes purported SEO experts will target websites that have not defined meta keywords and claim that their pages are not properly optimized, but you can safely disregard these warnings. The only reason you might want to use meta keywords is to reduce the amount of automated spam from these supposed SEO experts.

Text

The text that is visible to readers can also be marked up in ways that can increase the page's ranking for certain search terms. First, the most important way to optimize your text for search engines is to have the terms for which you wish to rank appear in the paragraphs of the unique content of the page.

Here are a few of the HTML tags that visually affect the text of a page and also impact its optimization:

H Tags: The heading tags, especially the <h1> tag, are extremely important. The h1 tag should describe the page. If you use the h1 tag, the font size for the text should be larger than that of the main content text. Do not define your h1 style to be the same size or smaller than the text of the content or Google will view this as a signal to de-emphasize the h1 tag.

If you use an h1 tag, you should only use it once. If you use the h1 tag more than once, you will not receive much, if any value. For the lower heading tags, h2–h6, you can use them more often, but at most once per 100 words.

ALT Tag (or ALT Text): Use alt tags for images. This is text that describes an image, so that if someone who is visually impaired visits the page, the browser will provide a text description of the image. Alt tags/text will both increase your keyword density for particular terms, as well as increase the rankings of these images in Google image searches. In most cases, law firms are not looking for image traffic, but it is a good practice anyway.

There are many other tags that add a little bit of value, such as <b> <strong> tags, title attributes within link tags, etc. Most of these are of minimal importance, but you can certainly add them if desired. You can learn more about these tags and SEO at http://moz.com.

Structured Data

You can add structured data markup on your web page to help search engines better understand the content. We will just focus on the address markup here and point to some online resources for further reading. Structured markup is still in a state of flux, so checking the online resources is important to stay up-to-date on the latest standards, and what is working for SEO.

The markup language terms that the search engines use are available at schema.org. You can tag content such as your address, business hours, reviews, individual attorneys, and more.

Using markup should make it easier for Google to understand what each of the elements of your page is. And although Google is pretty good about doing this without markup, Google has indicated it will start giving more importance to markup in the future.

One instance where we have seen a definite benefit to using markup is with the address markup helping with Google local/map results, particularly in cases where Google was having difficulty determining the address on the website due to a formatting issue.

You could tag your address as follows:

```
<div itemscope itemtype="http://schema.org/Attorney">
<span itemprop="name">Law Offices of Stanley & Stern</span>
<div itemprop="address" itemscope itemtype="http://schema.org/PostalAddress">
<span itemprop="streetAddress">1380 Pear Ave</span>
```

```
<span itemprop="addressLocality">Mountain View</span>
<span itemprop="addressRegion">CA</span>
<span itemprop="postalCode">94043</span>
<span itemprop="addressCountry">USA</span>
<span itemprop="telephone">650-555-5555</span>
<span itemprop="faxNumber">888-555-5555</span>
</div>
</div>
```

If you are using structured data, do *not* spam it. Google has taken action against some websites that have abused structured data markup in ways that were not relevant to the content actually on the website.

WEBSITE STRUCTURE

In order to be effective and provide users with the most relevant information, search engines have to collect data from a vast number of websites (known as indexing). Webmasters can help search engines get this information quickly and accurately, which can lead to a significant advantage for their websites over those with obscure or confusing information. This chapter covers a few of the most important ways you can ensure that your website's structure and design are optimized for search engines.

Indexability

Websites must be indexable in order for their web pages to appear in search engine results pages. If a search engine cannot access your website or certain web pages on your website because they are password protected, blocked by a robots.txt file, or not linked to, the search engine will not be able to include those pages within its index. As a result, those web pages will never rank well (or at all) in search results.

Links within the Website and HTML Sitemaps

Every page of your website needs to be accessible either directly from the home page, or from another page directly linked from the home page. Many webmasters opt for the latter option—often in the form of an HTML sitemap—particularly if the website has more than just a few pages.

An HTML sitemap is typically a list that links to all of the pages on a website and is structured according to the hierarchy or organization of the website. If your website has hundreds of pages, you can divide your sitemap into multiple pages and link them together. The key, whether you have a single sitemap page or multiple pages, is that every page of your website should be reachable through the sitemap links, and the sitemap should be linked directly from the home page. One added benefit of having an HTML sitemap is that some users may use it to navigate to a particular page that might otherwise be hard to find or buried several links deep from the home page.

XML Sitemaps

Another way to provide search engines with an outline of the structure of your website is through an XML sitemap page. An XML sitemap is different from an HTML sitemap in that it is not readily accessible (nor readable) to humans because it is formatted specifically to aid search engines.

An XML sitemap can provide search engines with more information than an HTML sitemap, which is why it is important for webmasters to have both types of sitemaps. With an XML sitemap, you can provide not only the full list of pages on your website, but also rank which pages are the most important and/or updated most often. Google uses this information to prioritize those pages and crawl and index those pages more often. In general, law firms should specify their home page, practice area pages, and any pages updated often (such as a news page) as highest priority.

To create an XML sitemap, you would create a file (such as sitemap.xml) that contains your website information and the appropriate markup, and upload it to your web server.[9] Afterwards, you need to notify Google and other search engines about the sitemap either by editing the robots.txt file on your web server and adding a line to give the file location or by submitting it via Google Search Console (see below for more detailed information). Google Search Console allows you to see how Google will be listing all of the pages in your sitemap, which can help you determine whether you need to make any adjustments.

Robots.txt

Most websites have a robots.txt file that directs search engines to crawl or avoid certain web pages. You should check your robots.txt file to make sure that it is excluding only files you do not want to be crawled and indexed. Mistakes made in the robots.txt file can accidentally exclude entire sections of a website, preventing any page in that section from ranking at all in search results. The robots.txt file is always at the top level of your domain, so you can access it at http://www.your-domain.com/robots.txt. It should look something like this:

    User-agent: *
    Disallow: /cgi-bin/*

---

9. The details of creating and using an XML sitemap are too technical for discussion here, but if you would like to learn more, see http://www.sitemaps.org/protocol.html. Most websites have their XML sitemap created within their content management system (CMS), but if your CMS does not do that, there are third-party tools that will create an XML sitemap listed here: https://code.google.com/p/sitemap-generators/wiki/SitemapGenerators.

Disallow: /captcha/*
Allow: /
Sitemap: http://www.domain-name.com/sitemap.xml

In the above example, the robots.txt file is instructing all search engines not to crawl the cgi-bin and captcha directories, but allow all other pages to be indexed. The robots.txt file can also explicitly specify location of the XML sitemap file.

If your robots.txt file is excluding directories that contain content you want crawled, then immediately contact your webmaster or website developer and ask them to fix it or remove the robots.txt file altogether.

Speed

Another factor that Google uses to determine rankings is website performance. Websites that load faster provide a better experience for users, so all else being equal, Google tends to favor fast websites over slower ones. Many factors affect how quickly a web page loads, including whether the content is static, cached, or being delivered from a database; the number of files and Domain Name System calls that are needed to render a page; and the responsiveness of the server. While you may not have direct control over some of these factors, you may want to consider switching providers or hosts if any one is significantly burdening your website's performance.

Google provides a tool that assesses your website's performance and will provide you with some suggestions on how and where to optimize it for speed: https://developers.google.com/speed/pagespeed/insights/.

Many suggestions, such as optimizing graphic files or server response time, can be very helpful and should be followed. But be aware that some of the suggestions you get from the tool may contradict current trends in effective website design, such as having style definitions in a separate cascading style sheet (CSS) file from main HTML text. Even the use of Google's own tools, such as Google Analytics, will give you a lower score.

Note that the score given by the Google page speed tool is not the same as the ranking in Google search results. Google has changed it scoring system periodically. But that said, the tool will often give suggestions on how to improve the speed of the website for users.

The bottom line is that websites that load faster provide a better user experience, and are thus more likely to be favored by Google. And this tool will give you suggestions you may want to use to optimize speed.

Mobile and Responsive Design

Currently 30–60 percent of visitors to law firm websites are using a mobile device, such as a phone or tablet, and that number is increasing. To take advantage of this significant audience, your website should be readable on and optimized for mobile devices. Google has started penalizing websites that are not "mobile friendly" in search results displayed on mobile devices. Because this can cost websites a huge amount of traffic, it is essential to optimize your site for mobile devices. There are two main ways you can do that:

Responsive Web Design (RWD)

Websites that have adopted a responsive design (see Chapter 5 for more on RWD) deliver the same HTML to every visitor. However, the CSS—a simple way of adding stylistic differences to web pages—fonts, colors, spacing, optimizes how the content is displayed to match the attributes of the device the individual visitor is using—this enables the website to "respond" differently on different sized devices. When executed well, an RWD website will provide an excellent user experience regardless of whether a user is viewing the website on a small phone screen or on a large computer monitor.

Mobile Version

Another way to make your website mobile friendly is to serve different HTML depending on the user's device, either dynamically or by having a different URL for mobile devices (for example, http://m.your-domain.com instead of http://www .your-domain.com).

In general, the responsive design option is a better fit for most law firm websites. Responsive design focuses on the user's screen size, which is paramount to the user experience. The only instances where a mobile version might be preferable are if the mobile version takes advantage of some extra functionality that is only available on one type of device, or if you do not want the same content going to users on different devices. For example, some firms choose to scale back content on smartphones because their analytics prove that visitors are not accessing certain types of web content on smaller devices.

Google has provided a tool and some helpful information about mobile-friendly websites. You can test your website's mobile friendliness here: https://www.google .com/webmasters/tools/mobile-friendly/.

Google's mobile-friendly tool is one you should take very seriously. If your site is failing this test, then you face a serious risk of losing out on much of your mobile traffic potential. Speak with your developer and discuss having a mobile website designed for you as soon as possible.[10]

---

10. Google has information about designing and developing mobile websites, including responsive designs here: https://developers.google.com/webmasters/mobile-sites/.

Secure Server—https

Web servers that receive and deliver sensitive information, such as credit card numbers or other private information, should use server software to encrypt the communications. The most common protocol for encrypting this type of information on the Internet is *https*.

Google has stated that if a server is secure—that is, using https instead of http—the content that is delivered from that server will be rewarded in the search results. As of this writing, however, no one has actually observed this ranking preference for websites on secure servers. It is possible that Google has deferred implementing this change due to the widespread difficulty webmasters have in setting up secure websites. Additionally, Microsoft's Bing experienced serious issues maintaining the ranking of some websites that had moved to https from http (although Microsoft claims they are fixing this problem).

Nevertheless, using an https server is likely to be a factor for higher rankings at some point in the near future. Webmasters should ensure they have properly configured the server for https and that any images or scripts that are being loaded from sources outside of the web server are coming from secure servers, as well. Some browsers will give users a warning message when a web page contains both secure and unsecure files, which is a bad user experience. If you are going to use a secure server, make sure every component of your website and web page originates from a secure server.

DISTRIBUTION AND EDITORIAL PROMOTION

Websites that are editorially promoted and distributed by others will tend to receive higher rankings in the search engines. This distribution can be by inbound links to the website from other websites or by social media profiles and sharing.

Editorial Links

Since the early days of the Internet, webmasters have used links to introduce visitors to other interesting websites. Thus, in general, a website with many inbound links should be more "interesting and authoritative" than a website with fewer inbound links. Google used this proxy for value as part of its ranking algorithm, known as PageRank.[11] Today, while links often still do indicate an editorial determination of value, they have also become components of schemes attempting to manipulate Google rankings.

You should *not* buy links and you should *not* sell links. Google has invested significant resources into distinguishing websites with editorial links from those with

---

11. Described on Wikipedia here: https://en.wikipedia.org/wiki/PageRank.

purchased links. Google has announced unequivocally that it will punish websites that have purchased or sold links.[12]

Even aside from purchased links, not all links are the same. Lawyers should focus on getting free links from high-quality websites, such as other legal organizations; government entities; and charitable, educational, and civic organizations, etc.

Lawyer Directories

Some online lawyer directories are high-quality and are good sources for valuable links. For example, both the Avvo Lawyer Directory (http://www.avvo.com/find-a -lawyer) and the Justia-Legal Information Institute (LII) Lawyer Directory (https:// www.justia.com/lawyers, http://lawyers.law.cornell.edu) allow attorneys to create a profile that includes links to their own websites.

There are a number of other legal communities that offer free profiles with links to your website, including LawLink (http://lawlink.com) and wireLawyer (http://www.wirelawyer.com).

Blog/Blawg Directories

Directories of law blogs, also known as "blawgs," are another option for getting legitimate inbound links. Justia Blawg Search (http://blawgsearch.justia.com) and the American Bar Association Journal Blawg directory (http://www.abajournal .com/blawgs/) are two of the best places to submit your blog for inclusion.

Other Websites

There are some other general directories that have editorial links to law firms, such as dmoz.org, certain bar association websites, and online yellow pages.

In sum, as long as you are not paying for the links—either directly or indirectly— and the website is reputable and law-focused, the inbound links can help your overall SEO. And if you are posting high-quality content on your website or blog, you significantly increase the chances that it will get picked up and linked to on other high-quality editorial blogs and websites without having to do any submissions.

Link Spam and Penguin

In the past few years, Google has been increasingly focused on reducing link spam as part of their Penguin algorithm updates.[13] If you hire a link builder that buys links, submits your website to hundreds of directories through link networks, or

---

12. *See* Google, *Link Schemes, at* https://support.google.com/webmasters/answer/66356.

13. You can learn more about Google's Penguin update at Search Engine Land here: http:// searchengineland.com/library/google/google-penguin-update.

uses keyword spam in the link text, then you may face a penalty from Google for these practices.

It is important that your links be natural. That is not to say that you should not submit your website to directories and other websites to obtain links. Rather, you should not indiscriminately submit your website to link networks and websites that primarily try to influence the Google search results. The Penguin algorithm is constantly evolving, so you will want to stay abreast of the latest changes.

Social Media

There are two types of links you can obtain on social media sites: those on social media profiles, and those involved in sharing posts.

Social Media Profiles

Most social media profiles allow you to add links to your website and other media profiles. From a Google SEO perspective, Google+ (G+) is of the highest value. You can add three categories of links to your G+ profile: your own profiles on other websites, websites to which you contribute, and websites you like, but with which you are unaffiliated.

On G+, for the first category of links—links to other profiles—you should add your individual profile page on your website, as well as all of your other social media and directory profiles. This includes Facebook, Twitter, LinkedIn, Avvo, Justia, LII, and any others where you are listed. For the second type of link—websites to which you contribute—add the home page for your website(s) and blogs(s). For other links, you might want to link to legal websites, such as local courts or representatives, and other local websites, such as universities or sports teams.

Facebook, LinkedIn, and Twitter all provide the ability to include on your profile a link to your website. While the links on these websites currently have no-follow attributes and thus no apparent SEO value, it is possible that search engines are taking the links into account or might assign some value to them in the future. It does not hurt to include them.

Social Media Sharing

You can also get links to your website and blog through the sharing and liking of your content on social media.

Google+

Google's own social network, G+, is their primary place for sharing links with others. Although Google's current plans for the role of G+ are unclear, it is still likely to be of value for SEO. When posting a link to a website on G+, be sure to make your post viewable by the public, if appropriate, or at least to a wide circle of connections. The more people who see your link, the greater the likelihood that someone else will share it with others.

Twitter

Google may rank a page higher if a large number of tweets link to it. This is true regardless of links on the Twitter.com website having "nofollow"[14] attributes placed on them. A web page can get a very strong rankings bump for a short period of time if enough people tweet or retweet the link. But even longer term, there is value in having tweets with links to pages on your website, as there are numerous aggregators of tweets, and many of them do not include no-follows in their links and thus can add SEO value.

Facebook

Posting public posts on Facebook will help with Facebook searches. And now that Facebook is including public posts in Facebook's search results, it is likely to become more important in the search world than it has been in the past. Facebook search will likely be especially important for localized business, so there is real value in posting on Facebook, even if the posts do not help with Google search results.

LinkedIn

Posting on LinkedIn will primarily help you reach out to other LinkedIn users. It can be useful if you are connected to general counsel or to other attorneys and are looking for referral business.

RESOURCES

This chapter is, in a way, a quick snapshot of SEO as of the writing of this book. We have tried to cover the key areas that are timeless, like high-quality, original, focused content, and some of the newer areas such as schema markup. But SEO is always changing and is much deeper than can be covered in a chapter, or even a book. Luckily, there are many online resources that are being constantly updated and also contain breaking news as to new search engine algorithm changes or features.

General SEO Resources

Here are two of the best general SEO resources:

---

14. "Nofollow" provides a way for webmasters to tell search engines "Don't follow links on this page" or "Don't follow this specific link." Google does not pass PageRank from links with the nofollow attribute.

Search Engine Land (http://searchengineland.com) is a great place to get an overview and instructions on different methods for optimizing a website. It is also great for keeping up with search engine news and algorithm changes.

MOZ (http://moz.com) is a website and online community that has great summaries, tools, and analyses of SEO. It also offers paid services that can give subscribers a great understanding of how their websites are doing and what improvements can be made.

Legal Web Marketing Blogs and Resources

Here are some legally focused blogs and websites that focus on online legal marketing and touch on SEO. Listed alphabetically after Justia's own blog:

Legal Marketing and Technology Blog by Justia
https://onward.justia.com

AttorneySync Blog
http://www.attorneysync.com/blog/

LawSites by Robert Ambrogi
http://www.lawsitesblog.com

Lawyerist
https://lawyerist.com

Lawyernomics by Avvo
http://lawyernomics.avvo.com

Mockingbird Blog
http://mockingbird.marketing/blog/

Real Lawyers Have Blogs by LexBlog
http://kevin.lexblog.com

Law Firm 4.0 Blog
http://LawFirm4-0Blog.com

Google and Bing Webmaster Tools

Here are the URLs of the webmaster tools/consoles for Google and Bing:

Google Search Console (formerly Google Webmaster Tools) https://www .google.com/webmasters/

This will give you additional insight to your website, including your search traffic, backlinks, and any issues Google might have with your website, including manual penalties.

Bing Webmaster Tools

http://www.bing.com/toolbox/webmaster

This will give you similar insights to your website from the Microsoft Bing perspective.

CONCLUSION

We recommend that after reading this chapter folks check out the online resources in the previous section. Finally, this statement is true today and will be true tomorrow:

Your website must have high-quality, original, focused content.

15

Choosing Your Consultants and Vendors

This chapter outlines all the options you have available when it comes to hiring outside talent. This list is not geared only to large firms—small firms have most of the same choices. For solos and small firms, it is even more important to hire the right consultants—you need a consultant who has a best practices approach. Hire someone—or some company—that has a track record you can verify and clients that really like and respect them.

The website developer options available today are nearly limitless, ranging from your ninth grade son who is a self-taught programmer to the large and expensive technology companies that develop sophisticated enterprise websites and e-commerce platforms for Fortune 500 corporations. What option is the best for your firm, and how should you choose? Given that this website may be your most expensive marketing, business development, and recruiting investment, it must be great—good will not be good enough.

ONE-STOP SHOP FOR WEBSITES

There are only a handful of one-stop shop choices with deep experience working with law firms. Most vendors are fine designers, but their technology is not state of the art. Or, they have that, but their design skills are lacking. And few are skilled enough in terms of what lawyers do to be able to write today's important content.

Look for companies that can help you strategize, design, write content, build, and host your website. One-stop shops are not equal, and the prices they charge and the services they offer vary greatly. Some are excellent, others are average, and some are downright poor. Interview these companies with your firm's goals in mind, just as you would interview any other strategic vendor partner. In working with these companies, insist that design decisions are consistent with your firm's key messages, and watch that they do not recommend an off-the-shelf or template look that you feel is not uniquely you.

Finally, go into this relationship viewing it as long-term. At least five years. The company you choose should be with you throughout the life of your website, adjusting it and enhancing it as your needs grow and change. If the company personnel have a strong service ethic and they perform as promised, they should be an important part of your consulting team for years, not months.

WEB DESIGNER AND/OR DEVELOPER

You have an infinite number of choices here, which makes the choosing both easy and difficult. Here are the questions to ask:

1. Do we have an existing trusted relationship with this studio or firm? A shared history of working together is not critical, but it can be helpful. They already know you, so your ramp-up time is less—time that you do not need to pay for.
2. Who are the web designer or developer's clients? A commercial law firm should ask what do their business-to-business sites look like? Who are the target audiences of their clients' sites? What if you want to sell a book you have written on your site—does the designer or developer understand e-commerce and what goes into providing a secure site for your visitors to purchase it?

    Personal injury and other consumer-oriented law firms should ask how intuitive and user-friendly the sites are that they have created. Will the everyday Gregg or Linda needing a lawyer be able to find you and the information they want?
3. How do they staff web design or development projects—all in-house, or do they outsource pieces of it (one is not necessarily better than the other).
4. What is their track record for bringing projects in on time and within budget? Ask for client references.
5. Do they know the legal industry inside and out? Can they help you with marketing strategy and enhance your marketing vision, or are they best described as capable geeks? (Ask for client references here, too.)
6. What is their philosophy about using the website as a positioning and branding tool? How have they demonstrated this? Have them walk through the strategy behind their recent launched projects.

7. What is their philosophy about using the website as a key business development tool? How do they achieve this? Ask for specific examples.
8. Are their prices competitive with the market? If not, is there a good reason why? (Note the comments earlier in this book that the cheapest price is not necessarily the right or best choice. But any vendor should be able to justify the prices they charge.)
9. Does it make sense for one firm to handle your logo design, advertising, and print materials, and another firm to handle your website?

Caution: Law firms often do the very thing they wish their clients would not do—they spread marketing and design work around. The marketing initiatives that involve producing brochures, websites, advertising, and other visual elements should be centralized and coordinated to ensure strategic consistency. Regardless of the medium, the law firm's positioning strategy should remain constant. This process and the result are harder to control if several design firms are involved. Leveraging (i.e., saving time and money) concepts, copy, and design is more difficult when messages and images are being created by several firms.

Choose a web design or development team that understands how far law firms have come (remember, law firms have been advertising since 1977). Say "No!" to any design firm that suggests a home or interior page with a collage of a Montblanc pen, the Wall Street Journal, and a gavel. This means they do not really understand the business you are going after. Stay away from tired images that say nothing about who you really are.

STRATEGY AND POSITIONING/BRANDING CONSULTANTS

Marketing strategists and positioning/branding experts are common in corporate America, but less so in the legal industry. They were more common in the legal industry pre-recession (from 2004–2008) than they are now, because, during the recession, law firms began cocooning—looking internally and focusing on cost-cutting. "Branding" almost became a four-letter word—everything was about business development, and traditional marketing initiatives were cast aside in favor of the hope that whatever the marketers did would drive new revenue. Law firm leaders lost courage and it was obvious in the websites that were designed between 2009–2011.

Of course, things are cyclical and law firm leaders are tired of their firms looking like all others. This is where strategy comes in. Some website companies employ successful positioning and branding strategic thinkers, but many do not. Whether your website company has this type of expert in-house, or you need to hire an additional consultant, invest in this foundational and critically essential component.

These consultants are familiar and current with legal industry trends and have a working knowledge of what is going on in your clients' industries. They know when clients need and hire law firms, and understand how they hire them. They will not let you go to market as "full service" simply because your competitor down the street does, or allow you to be so internally focused that you neglect to look outward. These professionals also will fall on their swords before allowing you to compromise the integrity of your firm identity, position, and brand.

Why is it ineffective for a law firm to focus inwardly instead of gearing messages to their outward audiences? Here are two examples:

1. Imagine a website lawyer bio for James Harrison that lists commercial litigation as his primary practice area. It also details all bar activity, articles written, and speeches presented. A prospect reading this has no clue about specific cases James has handled, or the experience he has in certain industries and substantive areas of the law, such as intellectual property or products liability. James has focused on credential building only, not on what he has specifically done for past clients and what he can do for future ones. *He is not making it easy to hire him.*

2. Another example is how firms present practice capabilities. As mentioned in Chapter 5, many firms organize their websites the way they are organized internally. Corporate and real estate might be combined in a business or transactional section, while labor/employment is part of the litigation section. If you present your practice capabilities this way, a real estate developer needing representation in your region will have no idea that your firm represents developers—because the information is not organized so that interested visitors can easily find it. Come right out and say "Real Estate Development" and include it in your main practice or industry list.

Hiring a consultant who can point out these glaring mistakes can make your job easier and your product better. Many firms do not have the luxury of having a senior marketing strategist in their employ—someone whose job it is to monitor the 30,000-foot view of your firm. If your firm is lucky enough to have a chief marketing/business development officer, often that person is involved in broader strategic initiatives, so he or she does not have time to also serve as the firm's brand and web project manager. In larger firms, typically this responsibility falls to a marketing manager, or more frequently today in mid-size and larger firms, a marketing technology manager. But, for smaller firms, a consultant is often the best solution.

It may be difficult for firm employees to firmly state the reasons for taking chances and making changes, and otherwise push the firm forward. A third party may have more success being the independent voice of the marketplace. As many talented employees know, it is hard to be a prophet in your own land.

COPYWRITERS AND COPYEDITORS

Refresh your content when it is time for a website redesign. Do not leave this very large task up to your lawyers—they are busy. Hire a copywriter who has significant experience in the legal industry, or at least writing for other professional services firms—this is not the time to educate a newbie. It is critical that the copywriter has a working knowledge of the law and what lawyers do. This will save you time, headaches, and money—and possible embarrassment in the event the copywriter uses legal or business terminology incorrectly.

Your experienced legal industry copywriter will know the difference between a tort and a torte and will have the ability to distill complex subject matter so that it speaks to your visitors. Website visitors are scanning readers—increasingly now that they are reading a lot on mobile devices. The tone of lawyer bios, practice descriptions, careers pages, etc., should be conversational. Tell interesting stories about what you do. Simple, short, engaging copy will keep your visitors coming back to learn more. Do not be afraid to inject personality into your website copy—remember, you are speaking to another human. Some web design firms employ copywriters who can become a part of your web development team.

WEBSITE MAINTENANCE

Your website development company should be responsible for maintaining your site post-launch, fixing issues and bugs, and making enhancements that involve design and programming. Your maintenance services will be governed by some type of maintenance contract or service level agreement (SLA), which will outline in specific detail a description of the services and the user environment, responsibilities, and support services available to clients related to the website implementations. The SLA should include:

- A discussion of the type of services
- Definitions/acronyms/abbreviations
- Description of the actual services provided
- Dependencies (what is dependent upon what) and metrics
- Non-emergency enhancements
- Scheduled maintenance
- Normal business hours
- After-hours access
- Escalation in case of emergency.

If you have purchased a site with a content management system (CMS), your law firm will be expected to make post-launch content changes—and perhaps image and other changes, depending on the features and functionality of your site and web admin. Large firms often have a dedicated webmaster—someone who updates the site when lawyers leave or join the firm, and otherwise keeps the content fresh. Smaller firms rely on administrative employees and even lawyers to make these regular updates.

Most top website companies offer maintenance agreements that provide design, programming, project management, and testing time at a certain stated cost. The fees associated with these agreements vary widely, ranging from a flat 20 percent of the total website cost per year, to something less—or more—than that. Consider these costs—and the important services the vendors provide—when selecting your consulting vendor.

Know that certain enhancements or statement of work changes will fall outside the context of your maintenance agreement. These will be additional charges, and should be agreed to in writing before the vendor proceeds with the work.

Look for both flexibility and predictability in your maintenance agreement.

SOCIAL MEDIA CONSULTANTS

Social media is a highly specialized area that is changing every day—new rules, platforms, strategies, and tactics. Being "social" is an enormous part of content strategy, which was discussed in Chapter 2. While there is tremendous noise, lawyers must learn how to sift through it, or, in this tiny sound bite world, they will not be heard. In October 2016, Twitter alone had 317 million users.

Remember what we wrote earlier in this book and what Eric Fletcher, the chief marketing officer (CMO) of Liskow & Lewis, says in the book he co-authored, *8 Mandates for Social Media Marketing Success*: "Any effort to develop an effective social media marketing strategy is built on a listening foundation or platform . . . one of the great challenges . . . is to resist the temptation to bypass the process of laying the foundation and jump straight to the sales proposition."

Fletcher continues, "The explosion of social media affords multiple channels that give you a behind-the-scenes ear on the conversations, concerns, aspirations and experiences of your audience." But, he notes that you must identify your target market(s) first—"absent this target identification, listening is rarely effective." The bottom line is that people "talk" a lot on social media, often without filters—take advantage of the opportunity to eavesdrop.

Lawyers—everyone, really—want to shortcut the process, and social media falls into that trap. First understand the platforms and what they offer, identify the people you want to reach, then climb in and participate.

When it comes to what kind of consultant to hire, Elizabeth Lampert, president of Elizabeth Lampert PR, says, "Not every law firm is set up with the expertise or bandwidth to handle social media internally, so hiring a consultant can be a smart choice."

So, should a law firm hire a social media consultant or a public relations (PR) consultant? Lampert says:

Sometimes what you need is just a solid PR/social media strategy and plan. A good PR professional can get that job done—helping you establish your goals, objectives, strategy, plan, tactics, timeline, get your team started, and check back now and then.

If you're already using PR and social media tactics, but in a disorganized way the same applies. A PR consultant can guide you, identify and analyze what's been working, what hasn't worked, and what has the potential to work in the future, and why.

It's time to hire a social media specialist when you want to take your social media marketing to the next level, and ready to devote dedicated time and an appropriate budget. That's when you need some muscle in the room and you want the advice of a true social media expert.

Oliver Thoenen, Senior Manager of Strategic Communications and Public Relations at Hinshaw, adds, "Hiring a social media consultant is appropriate only in fairly limited circumstances. For example, a consultant cannot—should not—take the place of an in-house social media specialist." (These professionals are more often found in mid-sized to larger firms, but small firms are increasingly hiring someone to handle social media in-house.) Thoenen continues, "Instead, their deployment should be targeted and limited in scope. Social consultants—as with most law firm consulting engagements—are best deployed when launching key new firmwide initiatives, such as an enterprise social media program or targeted lead generation program (a precursor of a sales program) using social media."

"There are a few basic principles that make social media work, and they really aren't that complicated," says Adrian Dayton, founder of ClearView Social and author of *LinkedIn & Blogs for Lawyers: Building High Value Relationships in a Digital Age* (West 2012), co-authored by Amy Knapp, and *Social Media for Lawyers: Twitter Edition* (ARK 2009). Dayton states:

> Far more complicated is selling social media to lawyers, who, in general, can be very difficult to persuade to look at things in new or different ways. And far more important than any other criteria in selecting a social media consultant is the ability to connect with and gain the confidence of lawyers. Lawyers will give a consultant about ten seconds to make an impression, and if they aren't successful, they lose the lawyer forever.

In Dayton's experience, his having a J.D. helps him to connect with lawyers on an intellectual level before he talks to them about marketing.

Advice from Others

Seasoned CMOs have seen it all—the cycles, time-wasting, and ramifications of jumping on the various bandwagons. (Remember TQM?) But "social" is here to stay, and its impact today is a fraction of what it will be tomorrow. It is critical to get it right the first time.

Below is how Allen Fuqua, CMO of Winstead PC, and Eric Fletcher (identified above) would approach hiring a consultant:

1. *If you were to hire a social consultant, what skills would you be seeking?*

   Fuqua: I'd ask these questions:
   a. Do you know how to stratify the various social media offerings, tactics, etc., based on age of the audience and their digital sophistication?
   b. Can you offer easy-to-execute tactics for attorneys to do social media?
   c. Can you help them target by industry and company?

   Fletcher: Some of this may be more "characteristics" than "skills." Four things strike me as critical:
   a. *Communication*—obvious, yes; but this is more than written and oral skills. It includes listening, interpreting, empathizing capabilities.
   b. *Technologically savvy*—Again, this may be obvious; but I'd seek someone who is comfortable with technology, yet doesn't believe s/he has "figured it out." New tools/tech solutions are inevitable. An excellent social media consultant won't be marketing a one-size-fits-all- *all*-the-time solution.
   c. *Perspective*—Are they able to see a big picture and connect social media to an over-arching approach to interaction, visibility, research, and marketing communication.
   d. *Demonstrated expertise*—There are a number of consultants out there who haven't "walked the walk"—writing about it, hypothesizing about it are easy. I want someone who has demonstrated a level of expertise in the real world.

2. *For what would you hire them? A broad strategy? A niche campaign? And what's the right duration?*

   Fuqua: Two things: Easy do-it-yourself strategies for attorneys across the firm, and niche strategies/tactics for industry and/or target-company based efforts.

   Fletcher: I would lean more toward a holistic solution; this may be a by-product of where I am . . . if I were sitting in an organization with a strong social presence/platform then a campaign might seem a more likely fit. But I tend to think one-off efforts are counter to what makes social tick, which is on-going relationships. Without a "tribe" you have to be audacious to garner attention. The timing required to see any kind of return on the holistic approach would be 6–12 months.

3. *What makes sense to outsource—and what components of social media must you do in-house?*

   Fuqua: Outsource content identification and aggregation, social media strategy creation, and tactical planning. Keep content/communication strategy and tactics (social media is only one aspect of it) and selling it as a good idea in-house.

Fletcher: Go outside for strategic guidance, a robust listening platform, technological tools/solutions, and leveraging content generated for a discrete purpose (turning a [continuing legal education] seminar into a blog series, a Facebook campaign, tweets, etc.). My bias is that social media is about relationships (versus a channel for dispensing info), and that relationships require personal involvement. Individual is better than institutional; personal is better than surrogate. In my opinion, the issue around this often stems from a narrow view of what social is and what it can facilitate. Viewed as a way to accelerate network building and nurture strategic relationships, social warrants personal, internal attention. If viewed simply as another channel for distribution, outsource it all.

4. *How is a "social media consultant" different than a PR consultant?*

Fuqua: The PR consultant usually just deals with traditional media (print/broadcast). Ideally you would have a broad visibility campaign, which would integrate traditional media and social media—and someone internally would be leading this and determining what expertise is needed and how best to integrate it. You couldn't expect separate outside PR and social media consultants to do that. They are typically specialists with very focused points of view.

Fletcher: Social, at its best, is about conversation. Executed by individuals (with clear strategy and some common sense), it can possess an authentic "ring" to it. This authenticity is in direct proportion to the degree to which the conversation reflects real listening. PR, in most cases, is about carefully crafting and controlling a message.

SEARCH ENGINE OPTIMIZATION (SEO)/ SEARCH ENGINE MARKETING (SEM) CONSULTANTS

Conducting a Google search for "SEO consultant/Minneapolis" returns 162,000 results. It is impossible for lawyers or marketers to know whom to hire in this sea of names. The list is filled with charlatans and reputable firms alike—how do you tell the difference?

Josh Steimle is a contributor to Forbes.com who owns MWI, a search company with offices in the United States and Asia (www.mwi.com), and comments about SEO topics. One of his readers commented on one of his articles: "SEO is surely the greatest con ever. Can anyone here tell me how every would-be Internet Marketer on the planet can promise every client to get them onto the first page of Google natural search?"

Steimle unravels the confusing tangle by offering four tips that will help you identify and hire the right firm:

1. *Decide what you need.* Do you need link removal, reputation management, a one-time SEO audit, ongoing SEO, link building, [pay-per-click] management, retargeting, content marketing, or one of the other 20 services SEO firms frequently offer? If you're not sure what you need, start by figuring out the job to be done. Do you want to grow sales by 20% over the next 12 months, or leads by 50% over the next six months? Is your goal increased rankings, or do you just need the boss to know that someone is working on SEO and then you can check this bothersome item off your to-do list? Have a goal in mind by which you will measure the success of your engagement with your SEO firm, and make that goal the center of your communication with them. If you can't measure how successful your SEO efforts are, you're less likely to be successful with them.

2. *Get multiple consultations, but keep it secret.* Once you know what you want, sit down with an SEO firm, in person or by phone or email, that seems reasonably qualified and ask them to help you figure out what you need to do. Most SEO firms will gladly offer a free consultation because they know by doing so they have a chance to impress you and win your business. This time will also help you to know if you like the firm and the people you'll be working with. By the end of the consultation, which may take a few days if the SEO firm needs to go and do research on your website and industry, you should receive a proposal with the services you need and pricing for them. Then, unless you're in a time crunch and love the first firm you've met with, go do the same thing with one or two other firms to have a basis for comparison. But don't advertise this. When you tell an SEO firm "I'm shopping around," or "I'm talking to other firms," this doesn't always make them compete harder for your business, it may make them compete less. This is especially true of some of the best SEO firms, where clients are fighting to work with them rather than the SEO firm fighting to work with that client.

3. *Get case studies and references.* The #1 question you want answered from an SEO firm is "Are you going to help me get my job done?" . . . Without being able to see the future, the best way an SEO firm can answer this question is to show you that they've gotten the job done for other clients just like you. If you run a self-storage company, and you talk to an SEO firm that has done work with 10 other self-storage companies, and they've all had good results, then that's a reasonably good predictor they'll be successful working with your company. If your company is unique and you need a generalist SEO firm rather than one that focuses exclusively on your industry, get case studies and references from SEO firms that have at least done work for clients with similar business models and similar "jobs to be done" as yours.

4. *Make the firm tell you stories.* A good SEO firm executes tactically. A great SEO firm does that, but is highly creative as well, and creative people tell good

stories. Stories also allow you to get a truer vision of what the SEO firm is all about. Case studies and references are like looking up someone's LinkedIn profile. You should do that before hiring an employee, but you wouldn't hire someone based exclusively on their LinkedIn profile. You'd also want to hear them tell you stories about their background, experience, and successes and failures . . . Ask the SEO firm how they were founded, what their best client experience was, what their worst client experience was and how they handled it, and how they've improved over the years. Even if you have made up your mind after following the first three tips, as you listen to stories you may completely change your opinion.

If your law firm is serious about SEO, this will not seem like a daunting investment of time. If you are just kicking tires, then evaluate whether this time and money expenditure is right for you.

WEBSITE REQUESTS FOR PROPOSALS (RFPs) AND REQUESTS FOR INFORMATION (RFIs)

Many firms painstakingly prepare and distribute formal RFPs to web designers and developers. While it may be unpopular to say this, firms waste a tremendous amount of time crafting RFPs, sending it to dozens of qualified and unqualified companies, evaluating responses and interviewing too many short-listed companies. We reviewed one large firm's website RFP that was 99 pages long and stated a high-end budget for $50,000. The most qualified firms declined to participate because the process was so flawed from the outset.

Do not waste your or potential vendors' time. Also, do not invite companies to participate that you know you will not hire (with the intent of information or intelligence gathering)—it is not fair to them.

Other Website RFP Don'ts

1. Don't give a response time frame that is too short. Thoughtful vendors will spend many, many hours preparing their responses—this on top of their current client commitments. Be sensitive to what is going on in their world, too.
2. Don't ask questions that are not relevant to the engagement, such as anything that does not help you get your website launched. Take a critical look at what you really need to know to feel secure in your hiring decision.
3. Keith Wewe, vice president of Content Pilot says, "Don't forget to include a process for vendors to ask you questions about your RFP, your firm or your working style. This can be done via email or a conference call—or both. Not only will this give you a glimpse into their thoughtfulness, or lack thereof, but it will also allow the vendor to clarify your questions so they may provide a better response."

4. Wewe also added: "In today's digital world, don't ask for many printed copies to be shipped to you, unless you really need them. It's environmentally insensitive and likely doesn't conform to even your firm's policy on green initiatives. PDFs and Microsoft Word documents sent via email are sufficient and have an added benefit of being keyword searchable."

5. Elonide Semmes, president of Right Hat, adds: "Don't expect a developer to test for every phone, tablet and operating system—even those with less than 2% of the market. If your firm is on one of those outdated platforms use this as a time to update."

6. Don't require that design firms include "spec" design. Semmes notes: "Don't eliminate providers who don't provide speculative work. You wouldn't provide a complete trial strategy for free without discovery and depositions." The American Institute of Graphic Arts, the nation's largest and oldest professional association for design, "strongly discourages the practice of requesting that design work be produced and submitted on a speculative basis in order to be considered for acceptance on a project." It has produced a letter that it recommends design firms use, which includes this language: "There are few professions where all possible candidates are asked to do the work first, allowing the buyer to choose which one to compensate for their efforts. (Just consider the response if you were to ask a dozen lawyers to write a brief for you, from which you would then choose which one to pay!) We realize that there are some creative professions with a different set of standards, such as advertising and architecture, for which billings are substantial and continuous after you select a firm of record. In those cases, you are not receiving the final outcome (the advertising campaign or the building) for free up front as you would be in receiving a communication design solution." For more information, visit http://www.aiga.org/position-spec-work/.

7. Semmes also includes: "Don't expect photography of National Geographic quality on a royalty free budget."

8. Don't have an unrealistic budget. Create your budget and prioritize the things that are most important to you to include within it. As noted in Chapter 3, law firm websites can cost between $5,000 and $1 million or more. Have a ceiling price and communicate that to your potential vendors. That alone might knock contenders out of the running.

9. Don't treat your vendors like a, well, *vendor*. Approach this process with the idea that you are seeking a trusted partner. Follow the Golden Rule here—*Do unto others as you would have them do unto you.*

Website RFP and Post-RFP Do's

1. Ensure that your vendor asks questions that really matter to you, such as, "What is your budget for this project?" Or, "What are must-have features that you want?" Or, "What is driving your wish to launch in four months?"

2. Ask questions about *how* they work—what is their working style? For example, how do they accommodate and align with *your* working style? Speak about your culture, style of working, and commitment to your clients, and look for responses that align with your firm attributes. Remember that you are seeking a trusted partner.

3. Keith Wewe suggests: "Include a schedule of your decision-making timeline. It allows your vendors to put place-holders on their calendars for specific milestones—and will be helpful to you when attempting to schedule face-to-face meetings."

4. Ask what the service providers see as the next major change in technology that will impact your new law firm site—for example, responsive design or multi-media trends.

5. Only invite two or three vendors in for the "beauty contest." These trips are expensive and time-consuming for the vendors. Don't waste a vendor's money and time if you are not serious about hiring them.

6. Prepare to debrief with your losing vendors. Smart company leaders will want to know why you went in a different direction.

Keep this process very simple. Do not waste hundreds of hours creating a site map or outline of features and functionality. Your capable website company will initiate discussions with you that will surface all your areas of interest, then you will be better informed and you can create a wish list.

Interview the companies and talk to their references—and view the references' websites. Spend the bulk of your time and energy planning with your chosen vendor once they are on board, not before.

16

Analytics and Measuring Your Return on Investment

You must track your website visitors. Period. If you do not, you are guessing about the effectiveness of your most visible and expensive business development asset. Analytics tools help you understand your audience, from where they are coming, what time of day, the devices and browsers they use, and the pages they consume and do not consume. And much, much more.

GOOGLE ANALYTICS

Google Analytics is a "free" tool that you can set up to track your website traffic.

At the basic, or standard, level, Google Analytics *is* free. There is another level designed for large organizations called Enterprise Analytics. Law firms of all sizes get by with the standard package, which tracks at least the following:

- Number of sessions within a specified date range. You can filter this information by hour, day, week, month, or longer. A session is the period of time a user is actively engaged with your website, app, etc.
- Users—the total number of new and returning visitors to your site
- Page views—the total number of pages viewed during the time period
- Pages per session—the number of pages viewed during one session, on average
- Average session duration—how long visitors stay on your site, on average
- Bounce rate—The percentage of single-page visits—a visitor reaches any page on your site and leaves without visiting other pages
- Percentage of new sessions—the number of new visitors

Analytic results from Google Analytics

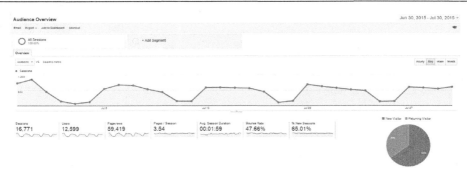

In addition, it tracks:

- Demographics of your visitors
  - Country
  - City
- System
  - Browser—Internet Explorer, Chrome, Safari, Firefox, etc.
  - Operating system—Windows, iOs (Apple), McIntosh, Android, Linux, Chrome OS, etc.
  - Service provider—such as Spectrum or Verizon
- Mobile
  - Operating system—iOs, Android, Windows, BlackBerry
  - Service provider—Verizon, AT&T, Sprint, etc.
  - Screen resolution—a variety of ranges that account for the various sizes of smartphones

You are able to dig deep into any one of these areas, seeing layers upon layers of data that will help you understand your website traffic. If you keep clicking, you will feel like Alice in Wonderland, ending far, far away from where you started.

An intoxicating feature is the "Real time" link, which shows you how many visitors are on your site "right now," their location, whether on desktop or mobile, and the top pages they are visiting.

You can also track:

- Top referrals—this details the top websites and links that refer traffic to your website, such as LinkedIn, Google, law firm networks of which you are a member, etc.
- Top social traffic—LinkedIn is a big referrer for many law firms. So is Twitter for those who are very active; law firm blogs are also a good referral source.
- Top keywords—what are people searching for when Google offers a link to your pages? It is very helpful to know what keywords are effective and top of mind for your visitors.

Real time results from Google Analytics

To collect such data, your developer must add the Google Analytics JavaScript tracking code to your website, mobile app, or other digital environment you want to measure. This tracking code provides a set of instructions to Google Analytics, telling it which user interactions it should pay attention to and which data it should collect. The way the data is collected depends on the environment you want to track.

Each time the tracking code is triggered by a user's behavior (e.g., when a visitor opens your home page and travels to a bio page), Google Analytics records that activity. First, the tracking code collects information about each activity, like the title of the page viewed. Then this data is packaged up in what Google calls a "hit." Once the hit has been created, it is sent to Google's servers for the next step—data processing.

According to Google Analytics:

> During data processing, Google Analytics transforms the raw data from collection using the settings in your Google Analytics account. These settings, also known as the configuration, help you align the data more closely with your measurement plan and business objectives.
>
> For example, you could set up something called a Filter that tells Google Analytics to remove any data from your own employees. During processing Google Analytics would then filter out all of the hits from your employees, so that this data wouldn't be used for your report calculations.

You can set up two Google Analytics accounts, one that includes your employees (perhaps called "Master") and one that does not ("Filtered"). To get a true picture of the level of engagement by visitors, set up both.

Google Analytics Academy (https://analyticsacademy.withgoogle.com) exists as a helpful and free tutorial for you. New features to these robust tools are being frequently added, with accompanying video and text tutorials.

OTHER ANALYTICS PROGRAMS

There are other fee-based analytics programs that are increasingly popular among larger firms that are seeking deeper levels of analysis, including Siteimprove.

Siteimprove (www.siteimprove.com)—Siteimprove Analytics helps firms dig deeper into who is visiting their websites—covering all that Google Analytics offers, but in a format that is more user friendly. Siteimprove is known for its Quality Assurance program, which uncovers needle-in-a-haystack issues with your website, such as broken links and misspelled words. Siteimprove Accessibility gives you a complete overview of your site's web accessibility issues, plus clear explanations of how they affect your users, and specific recommendations on how to fix them. With reports of one in five people in North America claiming some sort of disability, 20 percent of the population is a large group to ignore.

Siteimprove SEO helps firms that want to proactively manage their search engine optimization (SEO), offering administrative tools for things such as managing keywords and page optimization relationships. Finally, Siteimprove Response gives you a clear picture of how your site is performing, how fast or slow it loads, crashes, and other irregular behavior.

The cost is an annual subscription rate based on number of pages and yearly page views.

17

The Ethics of Client Development on the Internet and through Social Media

David Hricik[1]

INTRODUCTION

As of January 2014, 87 percent of American adults use the Internet.[2] And, as of January 2014, 74 percent of people who use the Internet also use social networking sites.[3] Studies show that in recent years between two-thirds and three-quarters of Americans use social networking sites, up from less than one-in-ten who did so when Pew Research Center began systematically tracking social media usage in 2005. Even among Internet users aged 50 to 64, about two-thirds are active on social media sites.[4] Although statistics for the judiciary's use of social media are less reliable, a 2012 Conference of Court Public Information Officers' survey showed that 46.1 percent of the responding judges used social media, with 86.3 percent of those that were doing so using Facebook and another 32.8 percent using LinkedIn.[5]

---

1. Professor of law, Mercer University School of Law, Macon, Georgia. Professor Hricik has written extensively about ethical issues arising from lawyers' use of technology. For additional research and information on the topics here, see, for example: David Hricik, Prashant Patel & Natasha Crispin, *An Article We Wrote Ourselves in the Future: Early 21st Century Views on Ethics and the Internet*, 1 St. Mary's J. Legal Mal. & Ethics 114 (2011).

2. Pew Research Center, *Internet Use over Time, at* http://www.pewinternet.org/data-trend/internet-use/internet-use-over-time (last visited Oct. 10, 2016).

3. Pew Research Center, *Social Media User Demographics, at* http://www.pewinternet.org/data-trend/social-media/social-media-user-demographics/ (last visited Oct. 10, 2016).

4. Pew Research Center, *Social Media Usage: 2005–2015, at* http://www.pewinternet.org/2015/10/08/social-networking-usage-2005-2015/ (last visited Oct. 10, 2016).

5. Christopher J. Davey et al., *New Media and the Courts: The Current Status and a Look at the Future*, 5, 65 (2010), *available at* http://ccpio.org/wp-content/uploads/2012/06/2010-ccpio-report.pdf.

Because so many people—some of whom are regularly participants in the judicial system—use social media, and thus it has become a central means for marketing and communicating, lawyers need to be aware of the problems that this common practice creates. Some of the ethical issues that marketing through social media and the Internet creates are not intuitive. This chapter highlights many of them.

Following the ethical rules is important, obviously, to avoid discipline. Discipline for inappropriate marketing is exceedingly rare. But the consequences of unethical marketing can cause more immediate harm. For example, it can result in negative publicity—not exactly what a lawyer was seeking—unenforceability of fee agreements, and loss of clients and respect in the community.

APPLICATION OF THE RULES REGULATING LAWYER MARKETING TO THE INTERNET

Most states have adopted ethical rules that are identical or largely identical to the American Bar Association Model Rules. This chapter focuses on the Model Rules, but it is important that lawyers make sure that the actual controlling rule in their state is identical in both words and interpretation to the authorities discussed in this chapter.

Determining the actual controlling rule can also be a challenge. After all, an Internet advertisement is "everywhere," so which state's law applies?[6] Clearly a lawyer should ensure that any marketing complies with the jurisdiction in which the lawyer is licensed. Where the lawyer is targeting a communication into another state, the lawyer should consider whether that state might apply its rules to the lawyer, and comply with the more stringent of the two rules.

Even if the lawyer is confident which rules will apply, and particularly on issues here, where there is at times very little authority on a particular issue, caution and thought are needed. Fortunately, many state bar associations also have "ethics hotlines" or advertising review committees that will provide answers to general questions about the rules, including those that relate to marketing.

The substance of the Model Rules that apply to communications by lawyers to prospective clients has been developed against the backdrop of First Amendment jurisprudence. Not that long ago, lawyer advertising was prohibited. That changed in the late 1970s, and today the law reflects the constitutionally protected nature of "even" commercial speech.

Today, the Model Rules provide detailed guidance as to what is prohibited, regulated, and allowed without restriction. The rules governing marketing and communication are collected in Model Rules 7.1 to 7.6. Most states adopt the rule

---

6. *See* Pa. Bar Ass'n Comm. on Legal Ethics and Prof'l Responsibility, Informal Op. 99-85 (1998).

numbers of the Model Rules, so the discussion about a particular rule number should correspond to the same numbered state rule.

Unfortunately, although collected in a relatively few rules, the Model Rules do not provide a checklist by form of communication, for example discussing oral communications before moving to written solicitations to advertisements in the public media. Instead, in some instances different rules apply to the same form of communication.

This chapter provides an overview by moving from rules that apply to all forms of communication (e.g., the prohibition against false or misleading statements), to those that apply only to specific forms of communication (e.g., written solicitations to prospective clients). After providing that overview for each rule, each section turns to how those rules have created problems for lawyers marketing on the Internet, including by way of using social media.

The Model Rules Regulate Commercial Speech—Only

The Model Rules do not limit a lawyer's political or other speech that is not directed toward commercial purposes;[7] however, the line between political and commercial speech is fuzzy, and it has become fuzzier. A clear example of commercial speech would be an e-mail sent by a lawyer to a person who the lawyer knows is in need of specific legal services, which suggests that the person hire the lawyer. But, is a lawyer "advertising" by blogging about an area of law, perhaps hoping that prospective clients will find his blog and hire him? What if he blogs in an area of political controversy that happens to be his practice area?

Lawyers who blog must seek passage in somewhat uncharted waters. Lawyers have been admonished for blogging in circumstances where arguably political speech was involved.[8] A risk-averse lawyer would treat all blogs and related communications as "advertisements" and not unregulated political speech.

Unfortunately, the precise contours of the boundary between protected speech and regulated commercial speech is beyond the scope of this chapter, and probably beyond the scope of any court to fully articulate. The point here is that lawyers should probably use an inclusive approach to what communications are covered by the Model Rules: If a significant motivation for the communication is getting clients, then it is probably best to follow the advertising rules.

---

7. *See* Texans Against Censorship, Inc. v. State Bar of Tex., 888 F. Supp. 2d 1328 (E.D. Tex. 1995).

8. *See* Hunter v. Va. State Bar, 744 S.E.2d 611 (Va. 2013) (engaging in lengthy, fact-based analysis of whether a lawyer's blog was subject to the Virginia advertising rules); N.Y. State Bar Ass'n Comm. on Prof. Ethics Op. No. 967 (June 5, 2013) (so long as primary purpose of blog is not retention of lawyer, it is not an advertisement); N.Y. St. B. Ass'n. Comm. on Prof'l Ethics, Op.918 (2012) (analyzing whether video lawyer posts to educate the public must comply with advertising rules); Philadelphia Bar Ass'n Prof'l Guidance Comm., Op. 201-6 (2010) (analyzing blogging issues).

A Lawyer Cannot Make a False or Misleading Communication about the Lawyer or the Lawyer's Services

There is no First Amendment protection for false or misleading commercial speech, and Model Rule 7.1 prohibits making "a false or misleading communication about the lawyer or the lawyer's services."[9] This Rule applies to all forms of communications, not only written communications. The Rule further defines a false or misleading communication as one that "contains a material misrepresentation of fact or law, or omits a fact necessary to make the statement considered as a whole not materially misleading."[10]

Of course, the Rule is easy to apply to statements that are demonstrably false. A lawyer should not claim to have graduated with honors when she did not, for example. However, the reach of the Rule is far greater than that. However, the scope is unclear. Until recently, Rule 7.1 listed five types of statements that were generally prohibited. It no longer does, but a few states continue to provide this additional guidance in the Rule. Now, Rule 7.1 in a comment identifies certain general types of statements that will, generally, be deemed misleading. Specifically, a truthful statement may be misleading if:

- The communication omits a fact necessary to make the lawyer's communication "considered as a whole not materially misleading."
- There is a substantial likelihood that the communication "will lead a reasonable person to formulate a specific conclusion about the lawyer or the lawyer's services for which there is no reasonable factual foundation."
- The communication truthfully reports a lawyer's achievements on behalf of clients or former clients, but it would lead "a reasonable person to form an unjustified expectation that the same results could be obtained for other clients in similar matters without reference to the specific factual and legal circumstances of each client's case."
- The communication contains "an unsubstantiated comparison of the lawyer's services or fees with the services or fees of other lawyers [that] may be misleading if presented with such specificity as would lead a reasonable person to conclude that the comparison can be substantiated."

Any statement that falls within one of these "buckets" should be reviewed carefully. Fortunately, the comments to the Model Rules suggest that a disclaimer ("Results are not typical" and the like) may make these statements permissible, but only if the disclaimer renders it so that statement is not likely to "create unjustified expectations or otherwise mislead the public." Include an appropriate disclaimer when in doubt.

Statements may appear on a lawyer's "profile" or other published description, as well as statements made by third parties that appear on the lawyer's profile

---

9. Model Rules of Prof'l Conduct R. 7.1.
10. *Id.*

page. Obviously, monitoring these statements is less of a concern on Facebook than it is on LinkedIn, Avvo, and other more business-oriented services. But even Facebook posts might create problems. For example, an announcement on Facebook of a jury verdict could, conceivably at least, be deemed to be stating the results of a specific case and thus be misleading unless it contains the required disclaimer. With respect to the more business-oriented sites, the risk of a communication being "commercial" obviously increases. Lawyers should assume that, if they are a member of one of these sites and post with the purpose of obtaining business, a communication must comply with the lawyer advertising rules.

Lawyers May Not Misleadingly Claim to Be a Specialist or Even to Have Expertise

Somewhat related to the prohibition against misleading statements is the general prohibition in Model Rule 7.4(d) against certifying that the lawyer is "certified as a specialist in a particular field of law" unless the lawyer has been certified by an authorized organization and the name of that organization is given. Obviously, a lawyer cannot falsely claim to be specialized in a certain field when that is false.

The Internet creates difficult ethical issues for lawyers with profiles on social media sites, and sometimes the answers to those issues are moving targets. For example, LinkedIn used to include a section on profiles labeled "Specialties." And LinkedIn did not permit the user to change or delete the label. The problem, for lawyers, was that using the word "specialty" could raise ethical issues. For example, the New York State Bar Association reasoned that a lawyer violated its version of Model Rule 7.4 by using a social media site that characterized his firm as a "specialist" because law firms cannot be specialists, only lawyers may be, and a lawyer may not indicate that he is a "specialist" unless he met state certification requirements.[11] Similarly, the Philadelphia Bar Association analyzed whether a lawyer could list her skills and expertise under LinkedIn's "Skills and Expertise" label and whether she could use LinkedIn's proficiency labels ("beginner" through "expert"). The committee wrote:

However, turning to the specific categories under that listing, in which the inquirer can specifically indicate that she is an "expert" in a certain field, the Committee finds that this could reasonably lead a consumer to believe that the lawyer is a "specialist," despite the fact that the lawyer's expertise does not invoke any of the provisions of Rule 7.4a which would allow such a description by the inquirer of herself. Thus, while the inquirer may list her practice area under the general category of "Skills and Expertise" the Committee finds that the inquirer may not categorize herself as expert or herself as an "expert" or for that matter "experienced" outside of the parameters of Rule 7.4.[12] Thus, the decision by a social media site

---

11. N.Y. State Bar Ass'n Comm. on Prof'l Ethics, Op. 972 (2013).
12. Philadelphia Bar Ass'n Prof'l Guidance Comm., Op. 2012-8 (2012).

to use certain labels for content can create ethical issues, and so lawyers should review the labels that a particular social media site uses to characterize a lawyer's skills or abilities for compliance with ethical rules. Further, checking for compliance once is not enough: LinkedIn, for example, over the years, changed its "Specialties" label to "Skills and Expertise," and then to "Skills and Endorsements." It is important to note that the structure and features on social media sites are frequently changing—often the bar associations are behind, publishing an opinion on a specific label or characterization only months after a change has occurred on the social media site. What if next week, for example, LinkedIn goes back to "Specialties"?

With Limited Exceptions, a Lawyer Cannot Pay a Person to Recommend the Lawyer's Services

Model Rule 7.2 prohibits paying anyone to recommend the lawyer's services, except (a) to pay for permitted advertisements or solicitations; (b) to pay for a law practice (itself subject to a rule); or (c) as a referral fee that complies with specific requirements.

The issue that online marketing creates often arises when a lawyer pays to participate in a web service that serves to match up persons in need of specific legal services with lawyers who provide those services. Whether the arrangement is an improper payment, or not, is a fact-based inquiry.[13] Any time an arrangement is exclusive (i.e., for paying a fee every prospective client in a particular zip code will be referred to a single lawyer), or payment is made on a per-referral basis, extreme care should be taken.

Synchronous or "Real-Time" Contact with Prospective Clients on the Internet and Inadvertently Forming Attorney-Client Relationships

For a long time, bar associations had struggled with how to treat e-mail, chat rooms, and the like when applying the rule against "in person" communications with prospective clients. Now, however, under Model Rule 7.3, a lawyer may not by in-person, live telephone, or "real-time electronic contact" seek employment from a person "when a significant motive for the lawyer's doing so is the lawyer's pecuniary gain," with limited exceptions.

The comments give no further guidance as to what is a "real-time electronic communication," other than to compare it to in-person or telephonic communications. Bar associations have indicated that chat rooms and the like are real-time electronic communications.[14] Lawyers should be concerned about this prohibition

---

13. *E.g.*, N.J. Ethics Op. 43 (2011) (discussing such a service and analyzing whether it was an improper referral service, among other things); Or. Ethics Op. 2007-180 (2007) (same).

14. *E.g.*, Ohio Bd. of Comm'rs on Grievances and Discipline, Op.2013-2 (2013).

when using chat rooms, Facebook "messaging," texting, and other forms of communication that allow for essentially contemporaneous responses.

However, at the same time at least one bar association recognized that the risks that may arise when a lawyer is face-to-face with a prospective client are not present in the modern world of Internet communications. The Philadelphia Bar Association stated that "social attitudes and developing rules of internet etiquette are changing," and so "it is apparent to everyone that they need not respond instantaneously to electronic overtures, and that everyone realizes that, like targeted mail, e-mail, blogs and chat room comments can be readily ignored, or not, as the recipient wishes."[15] On the other hand, bar associations also stated that "[c]ommunications sent to the profiles of prospective clients on social networking sites ... could be considered a hybrid between e-mail solicitation and contemporaneous communications one would find in an Internet chat room, as members of the social networking sites have the capability to respond to messages more or less instantly."[16]

Thus, until clarity finally occurred in a particular state, lawyers were faced with doubt over the boundary between permitted and prohibited communications. If they guessed wrong, they could be subjected to discipline.

Even if not prohibited, lawyers should be careful about giving casual advice in this environment. A lawyer who provides legal advice to a person about a specific problem has created an attorney-client relationship, with its attendant duties and liabilities.

Using E-mail and Other Asynchronous Forms of Communications to Solicit Prospective Clients

So far, the bar associations continue to hold that e-mail is not subject to the rules governing "real-time electronic communications." Whether, with the rise of smartphones and 24/7 access to e-mail, that will remain the case remains to be seen.

A lawyer using email to solicit business from a prospective client must under certain circumstances meet specific rules. Unless the e-mail is to a narrow set of prospective clients (former clients, lawyers, or family members, speaking generally), Model Rule 7.3(b) requires the e-mail to have "Advertising Material" at its "beginning and ending." What is the "beginning" of an email? Some states hold that so long as the "re" line contains "Advertising Material" the email does not have to include that phrase at the beginning of the text itself.[17] Not including the phrase in the "re" line creates the obvious problem that, when an e-mail is printed out, the "re" line arguably is the "beginning" of an e-mail.

---

15. Philadelphia Bar Op. 2010-6 (2010).
16. Maxwell E. Kautsch, *Attorney Advertising on the Web: Are We in Kansas Anymore?*, 78 J. Kan. B. Ass'n 35 (2009).
17. Neb. Jud. Ethics Comm., Adv. Op. 09-04 (2009).

In addition to legal ethics, lawyers must comply with state or federal substantive law. For example, lawyer e-mails that are sent to solicit business, directly or otherwise, may need to do more than comply with the ethics rules. For example, lawyer e-mails sent to solicit business from a prospective client may need to comply with a federal statute known as the Controlling the Assault of Non-Solicited Pornography and Marketing Act of 2003 and commonly referred to as CAN-SPAM.[18] The penalties for a violation can range from a few hundred dollars per offending e-mail to—theoretically at least—incarceration.

Advertisements on the Internet, Including Keyword Purchases

Advertisements in the public media are the least regulated form of lawyer communications. This is so because the ability of a lawyer to overreach is less if the communication is "passive," and also because unlike oral communications, there is a reliable record of what was said and by whom. The Model Rules require that advertisements meet the general requirements of the rules that apply to all communications, and also include the name and office address of at least one lawyer who is responsible for the communication.[19]

While it is easy to distinguish between a real-time communication and a static web page, those lines can become blurred on the Internet. A comment to Model Rule 7.3 helps to illuminate this dividing line, stating:

> A solicitation is a targeted communication initiated by the lawyer that is directed to a specific person and that offers to provide, or can reasonably be understood as offering to provide, legal services. In contrast, a lawyer's communication typically does not constitute a solicitation if it is directed to the general public, such as through a billboard, an Internet banner advertisement, a website or a television commercial, or if it is in response to a request for information or is automatically generated in response to Internet searches.[20]

Applying the distinction between targeted asynchronous communications and passive advertisements is often easy: law firm websites are not "advertisements," even though they contain keywords that describe the firm's areas of expertise. However, the Internet and social media challenge the idea of what is an "advertisement." A comment to the Model Rule seems to suggest that something is still an "advertisement" even if a lawyer pays a search company, such as Google, to have the lawyer's name appear in search results in response to particular terms (called "adwords")—say, for example, "expert in ethical issues in technology." Arguably, searches like this blur the line between a targeted communication to a person

---

18. FEDERAL TRADE COMM'N, CAN-SPAM ACT: A COMPLIANCE GUIDE FOR BUSINESS (2009), *available at* https://www.ftc.gov/tips-advice/business-center/guidance/can-spam-act-compliance-guide-business.

19. MODEL RULES OF PROF'L CONDUCT R. 7.2(c).

20. MODEL RULES OF PROF'L CONDUCT R. 7.3 cmt. 1.

known in need of particular legal services—which are subject to greater regulation under the ethical rules—and an advertisement.

One lawyer actually asked whether it was permissible to buy a search term that was another lawyer's name. The bar said "no,"[21] even though this is an acceptable practice to Google.

A special example of keyword problems arises when lawyers subscribe to a referral service. The New York State Bar Association Committee on Professional Ethics, in Opinion No. 799, concluded that efforts to match up a particular lawyer based on the client's problem was improper:

> We find that the line is crossed, however, when a website purports to recommend a particular lawyer or lawyers for the prospective client's problem, based on an analysis of that problem. For example, if a potential client describes a slip-and-fall incident on an intake form and the website determines that the problem calls for a personal injury lawyer and then recommends one or more attorneys in that area, the website is "recommending" those lawyers. This conclusion applies whether the website's selection of counsel is the result of human intelligence or a computer program designed to respond to certain key words (e.g., if the potential client uses the words "injury", "doctor" or "fell" on an intake form, the program would characterize the problem as one of "personal injury" in order to recommend lawyers). Such activity is prohibited by other than a qualified lawyer referral service.[22]

While obviously that reasoning should not apply to general search engines such as Google and Yahoo—since any search will result in listing many lawyers, not one—the use of referral services that utilize this method raise these distinct concerns.

RATINGS SERVICES AND REVIEWS

Various issues can arise because clients can say things about lawyers, some good and some bad. This section analyzes those issues, including whether a lawyer can encourage reviews or respond to negative reviews.

Providing a Discount to Encourage Reviews

The section after this one addresses what a lawyer can do when a former client posts negative reviews about a lawyer on services such as Avvo. Can a lawyer provide a discount or other financial promise to a client to encourage the client to post a review? Yes, says one ethics opinion—so long as the client actually writes the review, the discount is not contingent on its content, and the client is not coerced into doing it.[23]

---

21. N.C. State Bar, Formal Ethics Op. 14 (2012).
22. N.Y. State Bar Ass'n Comm. on Prof'l Ethics, Op.799 (2006).
23. N.Y. State Bar Ass'n Ethics Op. 1052 (2015).

Responding to Negative Comments from Former Clients

The beauty of the Internet is that it allows for instantaneous exchange of information. It is unrealistic to assume that every client is happy with the lawyer's work. If a former client posts negative information about a lawyer, can the lawyer respond by, for example, explaining the facts as to why the client is wrong or the actual facts demonstrate a different story?

Probably not. A lawyer may not do so if in doing so it would reveal information relating to the representation of the former client, and it is difficult to imagine how a lawyer could meaningfully rebut or address a former client's complaint without discussing some of the facts about the representation. Thus, lawyers may not respond to negative reviews—even false and demonstrably untrue ones—where doing so would require improper revelation of the former client's confidential information.[24]

Responding to Positive Comments by Clients

Suppose a client in response to a request by a lawyer to provide a rating or review writes something very nice about the lawyer—so nice, in fact, that it would be unethical if stated by the lawyer. What must the lawyer do?

Surprisingly, one bar association actually admonished a lawyer in that circumstance to "counsel" the client "about any omissions and advise the client about how the web page could be changed to comply with those rules."[25] That opinion reasoned:

> Client comments may violate Rule 7.1 depending on their content. 7.1(d) prohibits testimonials, and 7.1(d) and (b) ordinarily also prohibit client endorsements. In the Committee's view, a testimonial is a statement by a client or former client about an experience with the lawyer, whereas an endorsement is a more general recommendation or statement of approval of the lawyer. A lawyer should not solicit, nor allow publication of, testimonials. A lawyer should also not solicit, nor allow publication of, endorsements unless they are presented in a way that is not misleading nor likely to create unjustified expectations "The inclusion of an appropriate disclaimer or qualifying language may preclude a finding that a statement is likely to create unjustified expectations or otherwise mislead a prospective client." Cmt. 3.[26]

Another opinion went on to state that if the client refused to make the changes, the lawyer should "give serious consideration to withdrawal from representation to avoid any impression that the lawyer has authorized or adopted the client's continued use of the web page."[27]

---

24. *E.g.*, Pa. Bar Ass'n Comm. on Legal Ethics and Prof'l Responsibility, Formal Op. 2014-300 (2014) (collecting opinions that have so held).

25. S.C. Bar Op. 99-09 (1999); S. Ct. Ohio Bd. of Comm'rs on Grievances and Discipline, Op.2004-7 (2004) (same).

26. S.C. Ethics Advisory Op. 09-10 (2009).

27. S. Ct. Ohio Bd. of Comm'rs on Grievances and Discipline, Op.2004-7 (2004).

CONCLUSION

No doubt, not long after this book is in print, the Internet will have morphed once again. Lawyers should be careful when using new technology. They should read and apply the appropriate rules and, if in doubt and when necessary, seek guidance from the bar or an expert in the field.

Index